How to Predict the Future

A Revelation for Your Destiny

TERRENCE G. CLARK

All rights reserved. No part of this publication may be reproduced, stored in a retrieval system, or transmitted in any form or by any means—electronic, mechanical, photocopy, recording, or any other—except for brief quotation in printed reviews, without the prior permission of the publisher.

ISBN: 978-0-9889866-0-2 (paperback)
ISBN: 978-0-9889866-1-9 (ebook)

Copyright © 2003, 2012 by Terrence G. Clark
Published by: **The Glory Cloud publications LLC**
PO Box 193, Sicklerville NJ 08081
Theglorycloudpublications.com
Printed by Lightning Source

This book is dedicated to my mother, whose strong, relentless faith in God, and undying fortitude in life, inspired me to advance in life despite any obstacle—

Phyllis Loretta Clark
11.27.28 – 4.5.12

Joel 3:14

Multitudes, multitudes are in the valley of decision: for the day of the LORD is near in the valley of decision.

How To Predict The Future   **Terrence G. Clark**

Table of Contents

Introduction......................1
Chapter 1.....**Open the Door**...3
Chapter 2.....**Through the Door**...5
Chapter 3.....**The Unknown Truth**...*11*
Chapter 4.....**Who Followed Me Home?**...*15*
Chapter 5.....**It's All In the Family**...*19*
Chapter 6.....**Get Out of the Web**...*25*
Chapter 7.....**Panning for Gold**...*29*
Chapter 8.....**The Way of All the Earth**...*33*
Chapter 9.....**Can the Future Really Be Known?**...*43*
Chapter 10...**Prophetic Destiny**...*47*
Chapter 11...**Peace of Mind**...*49*
Chapter 12...**How Does Fortune Telling Work**...*53*
Chapter 13...**Psychic Phenomenon**...*59*
Chapter 14...**Is the Future the Final Destiny**...*63*
Chapter 15...**How Will Time End**...*67*
Chapter 16...**Can the Future Be Changed?**...*71*
Chapter 17...**Predictions from the Church**...*73*
Chapter 18...**Somebody Messed With The Soup**...*77*
Chapter 19...**How To Predict Your Future**...*81*
Chapter 20...**A Prayer**...83
Definitions and Expositions...*85*
Goals, Plans, Affirmation, Dates, Notes...*96-130*
References...*131*

How To Predict The Future **Terrence G. Clark**

Introduction

I have been in ministry over thirty two years. I serve as a church elder, bible teacher, pastor, writer, playwright, journalist, TV & radio talk show host as well as other like positions. Because of the nature of my ministry, I have been called a prophet in some ministry circles. Identifiably, I am a certified Life Coach (a field that even before certification), I have operated in throughout most of my life.

Conversely, I don't have a doctorate. Neither do I rest on my laurels of any other confirming titles preceding or following my name. In this book, I don't make any doctrinal, scientific, medical or psychological claims beyond my own studies and experiences. Having said that, the intent of this book is not to cure, heal or fix any illness.

This is not intended to be a religious book. The content is informational. Again, it is based on my research, insights, and experiences over the years. It is my intent, after reading this book that you (the reader) will be able to understand and make decisions that will help you change and predict your future. The information in this book is free. If you have purchased this book, you have paid for the process through which this information has been compiled and distributed.

I also considered calling the divisions in the book—*thoughts* instead of *chapters* because that term more realistically conveys the style and flow of the writing. Hence, the concepts introduce within these pages may be called as so—*thoughts*. These thoughts are not an attempt to create a new reality or entertain any existing dogma. These are excerpts that I believe exist in the frame work of creation and eternity. And, I believe they are confirmed within the pages of the holiest book of all.

Chapter 1
Open the Door

As I was walking on the boardwalk in Atlantic City one day, I was amazed at the number of fortuneteller booths and stores that were open. It seemed that on almost every block there was at least one Palm Reader or Card Reader. They were waiting for the crowds to yield at least one future-seeking tourist to stop in for a peek into their future. It was amazing to see the number of people who would venture out of the crowds with the hope of seeing the mystery of their lives unveiled.

Some were curious seekers at first people taking a chance to see if there was any reality to this method of knowing their fates. After all, the boardwalk was filled with high-rise casinos and casino goers trying to impact their destinies financially. A stop on their way to see what the wheel, ball, card or tealeaf would say seemed as an appropriate thing to do. Other people in the crowd were crowded in their minds with thoughts and choices on-waiting decisions to be made. Hidden information for a new job, old mate or life and death was calling out to anyone really seeking to know.

Perhaps, the fact that you are reading this book is evidence that you are a person seeking answers, directions or decisions in your life. If so, you have picked up the right book. At the end of this book, you will have found the answers you need. You will have found how to grasp those answers. You will be walked through a step-by-step process to help you know your future with clarity in a way you may not have ever known possible. You will gain the answer you seek without the use of a fortuneteller, tarot reader, or psychic. You will be able to exercise these steps in the privacy of your own home or secret place. Your life will never ever be the same again after this book.

As a further introduction to myself, I am essentially just a regular guy. I was raised in a Christian home. However, in my early teen years, I began experimenting with white witchcraft, horoscopes, transcendental meditation, and self-hypnosis. During this time something was revealed to me that changed my life. The desire to know my future, prophetic destiny and life purpose became a powerful motivation.

I spent many years as a young child living in torment and terror with terrible nightmares. I remember my childhood living in the country. Where, at night, there were no streetlights to divide the darkness. The darkness was so intense you could not see your hands in front of your eyes. Still, that did not compare to the spiritual darkness that surrounded night and day.

Witchcraft found its way into our family roots. I had a great aunt who was the family palm reader. Almost every family member had been touched by her soothsaying. Other brushes with occult practices were hidden in our family, such as the belief in old wives tales and the use of the Ouija board. All this was shrouded in the covering of religion. Even though professing Christianity, family members meddled in what was really forbidden by the family faith.

Chapter 1
Open the Door

As I was walking on the boardwalk in Atlantic City one day, I was amazed at the number of fortuneteller booths and stores that were open. It seemed that on almost every block there was at least one Palm Reader or Card Reader. They were waiting for the crowds to yield at least one future-seeking tourist to stop in for a peek into their future. It was amazing to see the number of people who would venture out of the crowds with the hope of seeing the mystery of their lives unveiled.

Some were curious seekers at first people taking a chance to see if there was any reality to this method of knowing their fates. After all, the boardwalk was filled with high-rise casinos and casino goers trying to impact their destinies financially. A stop on their way to see what the wheel, ball, card or tealeaf would say seemed as an appropriate thing to do. Other people in the crowd were crowded in their minds with thoughts and choices on-waiting decisions to be made. Hidden information for a new job, old mate or life and death was calling out to anyone really seeking to know.

Perhaps, the fact that you are reading this book is evidence that you are a person seeking answers, directions or decisions in your life. If so, you have picked up the right book. At the end of this book, you will have found the answers you need. You will have found how to grasp those answers. You will be walked through a step-by-step process to help you know your future with clarity in a way you may not have ever known possible. You will gain the answer you seek without the use of a fortuneteller, tarot reader, or psychic. You will be able to exercise these steps in the privacy of your own home or secret place. Your life will never ever be the same again after this book.

As a further introduction to myself, I am essentially just a regular guy. I was raised in a Christian home. However, in my early teen years, I began experimenting with white witchcraft, horoscopes, transcendental meditation, and self-hypnosis. During this time something was revealed to me that changed my life. The desire to know my future, prophetic destiny and life purpose became a powerful motivation.

I spent many years as a young child living in torment and terror with terrible nightmares. I remember my childhood living in the country. Where, at night, there were no streetlights to divide the darkness. The darkness was so intense you could not see your hands in front of your eyes. Still, that did not compare to the spiritual darkness that surrounded night and day.

Witchcraft found its way into our family roots. I had a great aunt who was the family palm reader. Almost every family member had been touched by her soothsaying. Other brushes with occult practices were hidden in our family, such as the belief in old wives tales and the use of the Ouija board. All this was shrouded in the covering of religion. Even though professing Christianity, family members meddled in what was really forbidden by the family faith.

Chapter 2
Through the Door

I was experimenting with self-hypnosis, which I stumbled on to through a magazine offer. The offer was for an at home course you could order. The purpose of this hypnosis study was to develop a photographic memory. The program seemed to work. (Even though, I now believe, continual positive, mental meditation and reinforcement can accomplish the same result.) I was able to walk into a class, take no notes and memorize the subject matter for the day. This really proved true when I had to take a memory quiz based on the atomic chart. Again, I took no notes and got a perfect score on the quiz the following day. For a period of time, I was able to sit, meditate, relax and allow my memory to recall information I would have normally forgotten.

The theory, this course emphasized, is that the human brain and psyche remembers everything it is exposed to, whether direct or indirect. For example, even a minute voice in a crowd of voices, gets recorded in the brain or mind. Even peripheral information finds its way to the archives of the cerebral cortex or psyche. (Some believe memory to be etched neural patterns in the brain; others lean to a subconscious idea of the mind.) The problem with memory was not remembering, but in a persons' ability to recall or extract information from the subconscious archives.

I was rather enjoying this newfound ability when one evening after school something unexpected happened. I was going through the mental activity that was a part of the memory course. I was lying on my bed, in my bedroom doing the visualization exercises. I began to imagine clouds, drifting through a blue sky. I was shutting out and tuning down any stray thought. It was in this stage of tranquility that you were to make positive affirmations of good memory and recall. "I remember everything. I have a perfect memory. I have perfect recall." These were some of the simple declarations to be made.

In the shadow cast of early evening light, before I could begin the positive affirmation, I began to experience a sensation. In my mind, I could see a spinning, spiral tunnel. I felt my mind move forward into the tunnel until I was caught in the movement. I was traveling around and around, moving deeper and deeper into the apparition toward the center. In a moment, I was at the center. At the center there was sense of passing from one place to another without moving. At that instance, I found myself with my eyes open looking around my bedroom. Actually, I thought my eyes were open. In my physical body my eyes were shut; however I could see not only through my eyelids, but around the room and through the walls. The dim-lit room now had a hazy cloud-like overcast.

I did not understand what I was experiencing. I was scared because I could not move my body. It was not so much as the feeling of impending danger, but the feeling of helplessness. I groaned trying to desperately move my body. I thought, if I could move, the experience would stop. I remember finally making my hand drop over the edge of the bed. Immediately, the experience stopped. I found myself totally unsure, but curious about what had just happened.

One would think that this would have thwarted me from the whole self-hypnosis process completely. But at this time in my life I was looking for some new understanding and insight into the spiritual realm. Actually, it wasn't the spiritual realm as in the mystical sense. I believed that there was a greater expression of life than the rigid tradition of my known religion revealed.

My interest was not out of disrespect for the fundamentals of faith and the Bible. It was not a problem with any disagreement of biblical facts, timelines or genealogies. The contradiction I found was with the dead teachings about God who the Bible declared to be living. I longed for the real and the demonstration of His written word. Unfortunately, dissatisfaction opens the door to the pull from forces of other things. These were things allowed into my family line by unknowing relatives.

My reference to things passed down through my family line is not to place blame on my relatives. An open door to the supernatural or metaphysical realm is readily available in the world today. In this day, the mystique and stigma associated with these things has been toned down. There was a day when practicing witchcraft was mysterious and forbidden. Those who practiced it were thought to be the weird and rejected. Witchcraft and other occult practices have now become more mainstreamed and in some instances fraternized. Also, introduction to this and other related things have been cleverly disguised to become more attractive. Exposure and acceptance have been partially due to presentation from Hollywood, video games, movies and books about children who engage in witchcraft as delightful fantasy.

Some of my other extracurricular spiritual studies included brief exposure to the zodiac. I also experimented with pyramids. I even tried to develop my extra sensory perception-*ESP*. I would sit in front of candles and try to move the flame with thought. I would concentrate on objects like forks and spoons to get them to move. I remember trying to read minds and project thoughts to other people through suggestion, in the form of *mental telepathy*. Again, all of this was shrouded and covered up by my dissatisfaction with the Baptist spirituality I was raised in. So I planned my next encounter with the tunnel. This time it would be in a so-called lab setting. I would do it with people around so if anything went wrong, I would have someone there to bring me back.

Present day, I do not recall what night of the week that I had planned everything, but it was to be downstairs in my family's living room. My mother and father, who did not know what was going on, were in the kitchen, around the corner, having conversation. The living room was dimly lit. I lay on my back on the floor and relaxed. I started the process—the blue sky, the drifting clouds, and then the tunnel. In a moment, I was in the tunnel's apex and was again looking through visual gates that were not my physical eyes. I could hear my mother and father talking in the background. This time, I was not cognizant from my eyes, but I was looking out the back of my head. I could see, perched at the top of my head, a figure. It was dark, baboon-like, potbellied, sitting and staring at me like a Buddha statue. This time, I was really scared. At that moment, I heard a voice. It was not audible; it was as if I perceived the voice. The voice said, "If you leave your body this thing (referring to the being sitting behind my head) will come in." Again, I could not move my body. I was more afraid now than at the first experience. After groaning and struggling, I was able to move my hand, and the apparition was gone, so I thought.

I later found out I had entered the beginning stage of what is known as *Astral Projection*. Astral Projection is the event of one's spirit or soul leaving or becoming detached from the physical body. This is a non-death experience. The spirit is able to view the world beyond the physical state. A person spirit or soul would be fully aware of its environment. Some have reported actually leaving their body and floating around the room. Others have claimed to leave the room and journey to other places or even countries. A conversation with one mother and wife revealed how she would often leave her body and fly around the room. What I later discovered (what the mother and many others do not know) is this seemingly harmless venture is accomplished with the aid of non-human, incorporeal beings called spirit guides or *demons*.

Chapter 3
The Unknown Truth

As previously acknowledged, although my family was Christian and tampering in the occult was taboo and inherently evil, it did not stop the shadows of darkness from finding its way to our family and neighborhood. I remember Christian parties at my parent's house when I was a younger. A Christian party, to us, was a non-alcoholic party with no secular music or dancing. There would be food, and games. Most played, were word and memory games. In the back room, where parents were not, sometimes a circle would gather and they play Spin the Bottle. Now thinking back, that was kind of weird, since most of the attendees were relatives or close friends. Although, it was not as weird, as the one party that someone brought an *Ouija board.*

An Ouija board is a game board with numbers, letters and words (such as yes, no, hello, goodbye) imprinted on it. A planchette—a wooden heart shaped object is placed on the board. Two people, seated across from one another, with the board in the center, place their fingertips on the planchette and allegedly allow an unseen force to glide the wooden coaster which has a circular viewer over the words, letters (forming words) or numbers that allegedly answers their questions.

I remember my attempt on the board. I don't remember anything happening then. I don't remember any movement of the planchette then. What I do remember is my brushes with the dark side afterwards.

Sometimes, innocence is the key to opening Pandora's Box. The statement "What you don't k now can't hurt you" is not always true. Eve, in the Garden of Eden, was innocent. She tried to rationalize with the serpent by misquoting and misunderstanding the command from God. God did not say, "Do not touch the tree," as she claimed (Genesis 3:1-6). He said, "Don't eat." Of course, as Eve, if a person did not touch the tree they could not eat its fruit, unless the fruit was brought or presented to them. In obedience, a person would not have touched the tree, but the fruit would still have been eaten. The consequences are the same. In that garden the penalty was physical and spiritual death. Likewise, innocent things such as the horoscope and zodiac draw you in like a spider's web, entangle you but contain a waiting predator.

Upfront, here is the key to the horoscope. It is not the words thrown together by some unwitting newspaper columnist to attract and to keep readers. It is the opening of the door called 'The desire to know?' It was Aristotle—the Greek philosopher and scientist who said, "All men desire to know." When there is a desire to know, all the devices from the external forces will be made available to make this happen.

Again the innocent proposition of playing a board game might still seem harmless and temporal, but it's to understand that no moment in life really exist alone. Everything is connected. The one night stand, for example, in an unprotected sexual encounter can result in several different and monumental life impacts. The quote "the sins of the fathers (or mothers)" is true to passing down its affect to the connecting generation and beyond. The dots of each picture are connected. When we retrace the manifest image that reflects back in the mirror, we may find that where that image began is lurking, hidden, further behind.

The connection between a simple board game and real life not only references cause and effect, but its points to influence. It's how decisions in the game and in life are made. As in the Garden of Eden, Adam and Eve were given all the trees in the garden to eat, which included the 'Tree of Life.' When we read the book of Genesis in the Bible, we find them standing somewhere near the tree of 'The Knowledge of Good and Evil,' which was the only tree they were not allowed to eat from. Conversely, they may not have been yet standing under the tree. The thought may have been introduced by the scheming serpent and presented to their minds, somewhere else in the story. However, there they are, close enough to pick and taste its forbidden fruit. The fruit itself may or may not have had some physical attraction, but its desire was more so born out of the improper rebuke of the serpent's contest, or out of human lust to try that which is forbidden. Thus rebellion spawned the phrase "the forbidden fruit."

It can also be accepted that the command from God was not to keep them from knowledge. In fact, mankind was created in the likeness of the 'All Knowing One' and possessed the capacity for tremendous knowledge. This knowledge was to spring from a relationship with Him and not a lustful pursuit, such as the desire of forbidden fruit. The serpent challenged and accused, "Doesn't God know that the day you eat you will become as gods knowing good and evil." If we would put ourselves in Eve's place, the question arises, why would we want to know evil? If we can live in a world where the good can be the reigning power and we can live our future by trusting God's goodness and dispelling any evil, why choose evil? The term "to know" implies not just to have knowledge, but to have a relationship with someone or something. We must determine if our flirt with knowledge will create a relationship with this knowledge. I remember the phrase "if you feed them (referring to a stray animal) they will follow you home." Whatever follows you home will soon become part of your life. If you feed and entertain godly knowledge and godly life, it will be in your house. In contrast, if you entertain and feed evil knowledge, it will be in your life.

Remember the phrase, "there is a sucker born every moment." Of course that's from the seller's side. The reality is that there are a lot of people, because of hurt, grief, uncertainty in their life, desiring to know what the future holds for them. We will discuss this in an upcoming chapter. Circumspectly, just knowing information about the future will not satisfy. In fact, it could create a deeper void and despair. Triumph is not found in knowing the future. It is found in the ability to control, create and determine your future and *destiny*. Success in life is not found in knowing if the glass is half-empty or full. Real success is found in knowing where the source of supply emanates. This reassurance also aligns with the thought, "When I don't know what my future holds, I can rest in the One who holds my future."

Chapter 4
Who Followed Me Home?

You may have heard this saying many times: "You must have been in my closet or in my stuff." Have you ever had someone read your inner most thoughts? Have you ever had someone repeat something you said in a past conversation that you were almost sure no one else was there?

I remember going to court for a traffic ticket several months later after the initial citation. The police officer that gave me the ticket was present. I was amazed that when asked by the judge to give his recollection of the event, he was able to recite word for word what had happened months before. I remember as he gave his account that it was as if I was reliving the day and moment of the event. Well this wasn't magic, it was a recording. The officer, having been there at the scene, recorded every detail of the incident. At the judge's demand he simply recited what was recorded at that incident. Also, in this particular case not only was the officer the recorder, he was my accuser to the judge.

Unbeknownst to most people, there have been reporters and recorders assigned to them at childhood. From day one, a host of these recorders have been sent to follow them around and record every detail in their lives. In fact, even without these reporters and recorders, every word and every thought of a human being is recorded to the letter and detail. The Bible says in Matthew 12:36 that every word a person speaks he must give an account of on the Day of Judgment. It sounds a little like being audited by the IRS.

There are different assignments of beings sent or assigned to an individual. One is from the dark side. The other is from the realm of light. We are talking about demons and *angels* and we will discuss them later in this book. There is also another recorder of information in life following a person around day after day. This individual records in two ways. This individual is the person himself.

Our life record is also stored within our brain or mind as we talked about earlier. The other way is through our soul and our emotions. Interestingly, information recorded this way is disclosed not only at the Day of Judgment, but often it is revealed indiscreetly, every day. The transcription of life's decisions will manifest itself in our behaviors and emotions. The choices we make in life will be read even in the way we dress and handle our finances. The Day of Judgment becomes not only a specific day in eternity, but judgments we make every day in our reactions and responses to the world in which we live. The Day of Judgment may also be how others around us judge our daily lives. The Bible states that people are living letters read by others—2 Corinthians 3:1-3

The police officer, being a servant of the law and court, could be called upon at any time to release the information to a judge, lawyer or someone else who knew the law. If someone had the ability or knowledge to call upon the recorder or reporter that was assigned to our lives, pages of information about us would be at their disposal.

A *cookie* in computer and internet technology is a stored message that identifies an internet surfer on a particular website. This information is usually willfully given and stored on a computer's *browser* until the person revisits the website again. When the website is reassessed all the afore given information of the surfer is uploaded. This gives the appearance that that the website visitation is personal for the returning visitor. A browser is a computer's application that allows the computer to search for and display web pages. It's what allows the texts and graphics of a webpage to be displayed on the screen.

There are small programs that follow an individual's internet activity. They track where a person has been on the World Wide Web. They track what websites a person has visited. This information is stored on that person's computer's hard drive until removed. Other computers technology can be somewhat more detailed and complicated. *Spyware* can follow a web surfer throughout the internet experience and report back to its host or creator personal data, internet surfing habits—recording trends and actions.

A computer *virus* can attached itself to a computer's hard drive and corrupt the system. A virus program will uncontrollably replicate itself in a computer memory arresting the system and causing it to crash. It can cause the system to run slow, or shut the system down completely. Warnings of the dangers of downloading programs from unfamiliar websites or opening unfamiliar email are numerous.

Sometimes things can get into a computer's operating system and it is not known where, why or how. The reality if steps are retraced, the origin, or the point of entry can be found. It can be the same in life. Sometimes people start experiencing strange activity in their physical life, thoughts, homes, or in the behavior of their family—spouses or children. This may be behavior or feelings that may seem unexplained or irrational. Depression, oppression, or lingering feelings of gloom in a person mind may be related to that same atmosphere lingering in their house. Restless children, a distracted spouse, or other explained phenomena may be the result of some (thing) that may have followed us home. These forces or entities attach to a person's thoughts, emotions and physical beings as connection is made with others in life or when unwarily exposed.

I was raised on my grandfather's farm. He raised cattle as one of his livestock ventures. So cattle excrement was in the fields all around. If someone walked into our house and the smell of cow manure pervaded with their entry, it could easily be assessed that that person walked through the cow pasture and stepped in manure. It may not have been intentional or obvious. En route, they were not aware of what they had tracked in or they would have cleaned their shoes. Ignorance did not stop the odor. The smell was related to the feces at foot and it affected the environment of the house. The person was before unaware, because of the open space outside and the fact the smell to some degree was common to the farm. When the odor was pent up in the house, its affect was more noticeable and unbearable. Sometimes the immediate effects of unwanted, attached things or forces are not known. However, their affect is just as real.

In all these examples, like my encounter with the court and the police officer, knowledge of my life (past or future) was not solely known by me. Others seemed to have more detailed information of me, than me. Like me, information (trivial or vital) on all humans is being collected by experts who record the details of our lives. The information is derived from places where we willfully, haphazardly or unconsciously trekked. It is recorded and calculated from things that we have done. Also, the fragrances of our life experiences, although sometimes unaware to us, are evident and affect the atmosphere around us. All it takes is someone who is able to read or interpret the data and play it back to us.

Chapter 5
It's All in the Family

A minister friend of mine told me of an experience he had in his pre-ministry teenage years. He was interested in a girl and visited her at her home one day. As he sat in her family room, a chair in the room moved across the floor. The chair moved without the help of any human intervention. The girlfriend, who was in the room, and had seen the chair move, calmly announced, "Oh, that just my dad." It was known that the girl's father had long been deceased. My friend's response was to quickly leave the house and not to return again.

You might say that this house had a family ghost or as what is known as a *familiar spir*it. There have been many unexplained events such as this. There have been many cases where families have claimed experiences in their houses or on their property as being the presence of a departed loved one. Investigators of the paranormal sometimes have ascribed experiences like this to the work of *poltergeist*.

There are other explanations of the wandering deceased. Some believe that these spirits are appointed to haunt until some type of closure surrounding their corporeal life has been settled or discovered. The Bible reports the common fate of all departed human beings. It testifies that once an eviction from the physical part has transpired, the previously embodied spirit or soul must leave the planet and exit stage left (or stage right depending on the destiny). Then what is the explanation to what my friend and others have experienced? What are these familiar spirits?

These entities are living devices existing to track you down. Some follow you home to the house to set up residence. Some are invited in. They desire to know you. They desire to know your family and become a part. Soon as they become a part, the control begins.

The 2001Hollywood movie, *The Others* was an excellent example. The plot twisted and reversed, plotting the incorporeal sprits as the dominate resident and the human homeowners as the intruders. In this script, it wasn't the human residents who exercised any legal right to stay. In film or real life, somewhere the premise has to be set and it has to be decided who is the protagonist and antagonist. Good and evil do not dwell together in harmony. Like any other home infestation, uninvited guest in a house are supposed to be exterminated.

I have seen entertainers at magic shows and circuses who set on their lap a dummy and project their voice through this puppet. Realistically speaking, the voice was not actually projected through the dummy, but it was projected *somewhere* to a place, where the sound and movement of the puppet mouth gave the appearance of speech. In fact, we have been programmed to watch whole shows, movies and animation where the projection was not real. So what if another entity caused an appearance of a departed person? We might unknowingly assume or believe that the apparition was someone who was not really there. This, however, does not disclaim the idea of the familiar (family) spirit. The perpetrator will stay until not welcomed and told to go. Until then it becomes the shadowed member of a household or someone's life.

Why the hoax? Again, one of the greatest entertainers once said, "there is a sucker born every minute." Sucker for what? A sucker will give up his life, money, ambitions, dreams and eternity for a lie or fantasy. How could or why would one give eternity away? Ask the fly caught in the spider's web. It looked pretty and empty. But every movement of the fly caused it to become more entrapped. Every movement got more attention from the waiting spider and eventually caused the fly to have its lifeblood sucked out. Perhaps the hoax is to lead the audience astray from the real picture. If the future is no more than unanswered flashes of light and unexplained moving objects, then there is no real reason to make confident decisions. If confident decisions are those that shape and affect our destiny, then we need to be sure of that destiny. Also, if we believe that destiny and eternity are not decisive things in this life, we may ignore those opportunities to choose when they are presented.

Life is a thing of purpose. It is in life we find and fulfill our purpose and make decision based on our purpose. Everyone has a purpose. It is part the great plan of life—the great design. There are over seven billion people in the world (at the release time of this book). Each life in that number has been created to help someone else in that number to fulfill theirs. It's the divine plan.

I sometimes hear ghost stories and wonder what the purpose of the encounter was? Why does the chair rock or why the apparition of Kernel Smith who died seven hundred years ago. Some people are entertained by ghostly events and others are terrified. The purpose is the distraction. The attainment of life purpose is based on who you worship. Who is the center of your life? Who is the center of your household? A ghost or the illusion of the departed comes to gain worship in a family. If there is something moving in the house or village it is to that thing that the house or village will give its attention.

When fear (negative worship) is the result of a ghostly encounter, this terrifying spirit tries to interrupt a home, life or family. Why? It's coming for worship. God—the great God of heaven is the only one to be worshipped and a wayfaring spirit tempts to bring that glory to itself. Even if the encounter is seemingly friendly, as with the familiar father spirit, it is still worship extended to an entity other than The Creator Himself.

A ghost represents an empty promise. People live in bodies on the earth. It's in a body that we live and have relationship and fulfill lives. In the 1990 Hollywood movie *Ghost*, *Patrick Swayze's* character is murdered and in spirit tries throughout the movie to connect to his girlfriend played by *Demi Moore*. He can't on his own, so finds a failing psychic played by *Whoopie Goldberg*. He is able to communicate to her (the psychic) and uses her to communicate to his wife. He also, through the psychic, resolves his death and brings to justice—his murderers. At the end of the movie, he possesses Whoopie's character and is able to have a tender final moment of resolution with his fiancée.

Swayze's character's good spirit is then ushered to a realm of peace, tranquility and joy, demonstrated in the movie by the warm light and angelic tones that surrounded his departure. The evil characters in the movie who die are portrayed as to being taken to another realm of darkness, as dark demon like figures come to pull their souls downward.

This is a pretty good enactment from Hollywood's view. The problem is what was perceived as good and evil from a human stand point may not be what the Judge of the universe has to say. The script also gave no absolutes. What was or is too evil for Heaven and what was or is good enough to miss Hell.

According to the bible, the moment someone leaves their body, through death, they are immediately sent to either Heaven or Hell (main stream interpretation). There is no in between. Hence the deception, if spirits are allowed to wonder aimlessly or purposely on earth after departure from the body, then the Bible is not true and there are no absolutes to access the world beyond.

According to the Bible, the greatest fulfillment of life and relationship is from the one who, came from heaven and lived in a human body (His own), was crucified in that body, came back to life in that body, went back to heaven in that body and is coming again for His family in that same body. It's this individual that although we cannot see now in the flesh that we put faith in. Again, He is in a body. This individual is Jesus Christ.

There is also a spirit that is now on the earth that wants access into our lives and our families, He is called the Holy Ghost, but He comes by invitation, only to those who have received Jesus Christ. Although, He has been known to show up and manifest the Love of God in places that He chooses and wills.

Adam and Eve in the Garden of Eden had a visitation from an illegal spirit who had possessed a snake. It was bad move on the part of the snake. We don't know how long the snake was allowed to hang around before they ate the forbidden fruit. We do know it was long enough for its presence to cause affect. The serpent, Satan, became a familiar spirit in the garden which was their home.

Hollywood heightened the ugly of the demonic and ghostly visitation. Some of the portrayals were based on truth. But after the fear of the demonic voice from the little girl and the rest of the ugly, what was left beyond the door. In movies like the *Exorcist* and the *Amityville Horror* some encounters with familiar sprits have been violent. In the book of Acts (Chapter 19), in the Bible, there were seven Jewish exorcist who tried to exercise a demon, but did not have the power and the authority given by Jesus Christ to believers to do so. The demonic spirit, possessing the person they were ministering to, jumped on them and sent them running—bleeding and naked out of the house. Interestingly, in the movies, whether based on a true story or not, the goal of the spirit visitation to that home was to gain the worship of the movie audience. The goal was to create the perception, in the mind of the representative of each house in the theater, that the ghost, demon or the devil himself was so powerful and could not be made to leave. If this thought can be entertained from the screen of the theater, it can give way to allow the visita-tion or other demonic affects in the homes or minds of the patrons.

Like the snake in the Garden, the visitations ultimate purpose was to bring thoughts. The primarily purpose of the presence of any kind of spirit is to bring thoughts to the human host. The thoughts are to be received or denied by the human host. It the purpose of the demonic to thwart an individual from the purpose of God and hindered them from fulfilling their destiny.

Again, in Adam and Eve's case it was to turn Adam's family and ultimately the whole family of the human race from God. The thought came to get them to doubt God's love for them and entertain the serpent's proposition under that tree—in their house.

The entrance of thoughts, as a familiar spirit, are more detrimental and affecting then the chair moving seeming by itself, or by the return of a departed soul. Families can have negative thoughts or behaviors lurking not only in their house, but visiting their whole family line. These are spirits whose strongholds have stemmed from a families roots (and history) and have gone unseen. However their affect are even greater than that which moved a chair or an unexplained cold chill in the room.

Chapter 6
Get Out Of The Web

I remember when I was about twelve or thirteen years old. I was running down the path to my cousin's house down the street. It was foggy this particular morning and I decided to run through some trees that grew together in his back yard. I had run that way many times before. However this day something different was there. Unseen to me in my haste and in the fog, a spider had spun a rather large web between the trees to capture prey. I was probably a little bigger than what it expected. The web did not catch me, but it did manage to go with me. I was covered with strands of polymer laced with dust and leaves. I remember knocking and shouting at my cousin's door as he and his mom opened it and stared. I remember yelling, as I tore the sticky filament off me (as they joined in), "Get it off of me. Get it off of me."

Sometimes the paths in life you take may be strewn with experiences, events and temptations that you didn't expect. Things may actually, in one sense, lay and wait for you. Some things may have been the plight awaiting someone else, but there you are. You are caught in a web, like the one designed for bugs, which entangled me. A prostitute or a pimp may tell their prospect that they have been waiting totally for them, but it's clear the first person around the corner who was willing to pay was the target. A mugger sometimes is looking for a particular person to pass the alley, but desperation may choose whoever walks his way. It may seem that destiny or opportunity may have put you on a particular course where some plan, device or trap may have purposely been set for you. You may find yourself in an environment or situation that you had not planned. Don't stop and immediately accept that as the fate of your life. Even if you have to keep running, taking the trap with you. If you run into a web of trouble on your path, don't get stopped by it, and get it off you. If needed, get help to get it off of you. Remember, whatever spun the web may still be there.

The Bible says the love of money is the root of all evil, not money, but the love of it. There are a lot of things done out of this love of money. People services like fortunetellers (from every discipline) that claim to really care about you may really have a hidden agenda. The depth of your wallet or purse may be the driving factor. There is no crime for charging for a service rendered, but when there is no true product or true help, therein lays the deception. The love of your wallet is the human side. There are forces that don't really care about your money. That is, they don't want to possess it. The goal of these forces is to steal something you own more precious and lasting than your money, your human soul.

People who are seeking to find their future or destiny and have sought it through the predictions of another are to be cautious, especially if they have not been told that they have the power to change and determine the outcome of their future. Jesus said, "If a man builds his house upon the sand, he will lose it to the wind and storms of life." It will fall no matter how secure the outer structure seems to be. It will fall no matter how comfy, cozy, homey, and inviting the interior seems to be. In contrast, the person who builds his house upon a rock, which is the Word of Jesus the Savior, will stand the test of all the fury of the trials of life. The ability to stand was not in knowing the forecast that wind was coming. The house stood because it had the right foundation (or substance) to stand in the midst of a threatening environment. Again, predicting the future was really the assurance of having built around you the things that will stand the test of time.

There is help given to us to overcome in life. The most powerful is the Rock of Christ—the Word of God which is called scripture. The word *scripture,* which means writings, is from the Greek word *graphe.* From this, we get the English word—*graphics.* Graphics are drawings or blue prints that are penned, inked or engraved. They produce a picture or an image. Graphics can also be etchings that are carved or burned into metal or stone. Civilizations from the past painted, etched or carved writing and pictures into wood and rock. Moses received God's Word etched, engraved or written into tables of stone. Hence, these tablet writings became scripture.

The force God used to etch into these stones had to be like that of a *laser.* Laser is concentrated light. A laser is directed light. It's light on a mission. God's light is still on a mission today to etch His Word in the hearts of men (male or female). When God's Word is etched into a person's heart it becomes like spiritual computer programming. It demands the surrounding environment to conform to what it said. It causes harmful strongholds from negative and evil entities in our life to be exposed. When they are exposed they lose their hold on us.

When a revelation of a truth comes and is realized, the power to resist and walk free of a lie (another stronghold) is present also. A circus elephant's leg is tied to a pole when he is a calf to condition him to stay put when he is a full grown. The rope or chain cannot really contain the five ton fully grown creature, but he doesn't know it. A dog who has been tied to a pole since a puppy may not realize when the rope leash, that has held him for years, has rotted. So he will stay put making the same circle in the backyard. When it finally realizes, by a two step romp beyond his normal circle without resistance, the dog will most likely run free. The outcome is the same whether in the analogy of a web or a leash. It may prove interesting biology or behavioral science when talking about bugs, dogs and elephants, but when people are the object or the victim it becomes life burdening, dream stealing and future robbing.

It's like the people on the boardwalk stopping in to get their fortunes told. It's like the person waiting to see what the daily horoscope says. It's like the two children sitting at the seemingly harmless disk of the Ouija board, the web has been strung. However, this may not be a cobweb but one with a waiting predator. Most people are innocent as they stumble upon these predatory traps. They may not necessarily get stopped immediately by the trap, but they may take the trap with them. It may not be apparent in the fog, trees or the dark, but exposure to the light will reveal it. At the end of this book there is a course of action to get out of the web of problems. These are the problems that are set, to get you off track and then drain your life's blood. This web includes the strands of fear, oppression, depression, torment, hopelessness and suicide.

Chapter 7
Panning for Gold, The Divining Rod And Becoming a Millionaire

I wrestled with the use of the following illustrations because of the appearance that I am endorsing them, I am not. The reference is merely because these methods of future prediction have been used by people--- particularly, the reference to water induction. I hope that rather it is seen as our attempt to distill the lore.

Younger readers may not be familiar with the term "panning for gold." This is the process of dipping a pan-shaped sieve into the bed of a river flowing from a mountain. The expectation is that gold on that mountain would be contained in the water. The panning process will gather into one swoop the sand, dirt and whatever else. The pan is then sifted to expose, reveal, and leave behind that which might have been hidden.

The *divining* rod is a "Y" shaped stick or branch (used by one who was accustomed to divining) to locate hidden reservoirs of water. The stick (allegedly) would pull the individual in the direction of the water and then vibrate to indicate when it was found.

The reference to panning for gold, as in predicting your future, is the process of sifting through the sand and water of the human soul. There are deposits inside every person's being. There is also chaff and refuse that has been deposited by the world. (The world is the system of human, spiritual, and societal influence. Further defined, it is the political, sociological and religious influence that governs planet Earth. It is also categorized as the lifestyle pattern that is opposite and contrary to the lifestyle that is obedient to God.) This chaff and refuse are things positive and negative added through the course of life. At birth or even before birth there was a deposit of gold and precious treasure laid. God has infused in the DNA of every child—his likeness. Every human born has the potential to be an active child of God. This reality exists just because humans are the off spring of Adam who God created in His image and likeness. Although flawed and corrupted by sin (disobedience), God has provided a way for all to be reborn into a new being. When one embraces a saving relationship with God through *Sonship* (that is relationship with God through Jesus Christ), access to that deposit has been given. However, even then, there needs to be a panning process to sift out and let the gold appear. Everyone has greatness in them. Everyone has the billionaire potential in him or her.

    To truly pan for gold is to pan for the gold inside yourself. When you truly find it, you may find that this gold—is you. The secret of obtaining gold is that first—it has to be found. The gold that is displayed, worn, or held in a safe as a wealth investment did not come out of the earth that way. There is a process. The gold must be separated from other materials that are bonded to it. This fusion of substances is sometimes pulverized into sand and separated first by water. Secondly it is melted by great heat. Thirdly, it is smelted—chemicals or other substances are added to the molten mix so that the gold can be purified. Reemphasizing, gold does not exist in nature in a refined stage. God alone is the purifier of the gold of the human life. The prospect of who each individual is or who they are to become is seen through His eyes.

    Unfortunately, many times, people long after someone else's life. Fans of celebrities compare themselves to their favorite actor, actress, musician, singer or sports player. Aspirations are often measured by the success of someone else's dream. Young girls and guys going wild at a music concert sometimes lower their morals under the shadow of some celebrity's image. Often forgotten is that the human star is also flawed and in need of rebirth. Images that are seen on TV, in the theater, or from the stadium are illuminated by that which surrounds them—the lights, the money, the music, the spirits and the fan themselves. When our thoughts are focused on someone else other than the Highest—the one who created us, we can never be the gold in life we were destined to be. Therefore panning on the outside is futility. Panning on the inside of a born again human spirit is to seek after the Creator Himself. The creation is only complete in the revelation of (and a relationship with) the Creator. How much the human soul is worth is a question pondered by philosophers. The Bible clarifies. Despite the worth it was before, its worth has been revalued. The worth is based on the cost paid by the purchaser. God purchased the human soul with the life of His only Son.

Again, I am going out on a limb in this comparison of the divining rod. I am not authenticating or endorsing this mystical method of looking for water. However, sometimes things that exist in legend, folklore and some non-biblical circles may be a perversion from spiritual truth. There is a branch of a different kind. In the Bible, Jesus Christ is called the branch (Isaiah 11:1, Jeremiah 23:5). He provides the way to a divine (not H_2O) living well of water inside a person's spirit and soul. He is also the source of the well. Inside this well lives the potential for greatness. Inside this well is the very flow of eternal destiny itself. It is a well of refreshment. It is a well of Life.

So by Christ, who is Life, we seek for Christ, and we will find Christ. When we find Christ, we find out that it is He who is reaching out for us (Christ is not lost). It is his desire for us that sparks or primes our desire for him. Just as there is no substitute that can satisfy thirst like water, satisfaction in life can only come from the one who satisfies us with his life.

When I was child, no one ever told me I could become a millionaire by thirty or forty years old if I put some basic investing principles in motion. No one told me it was my will, creativity, and faith in God, not necessarily my education that would cause me to be a success in life. What schoolteacher ever said life was not based on the analysis or report of a doctor, but again by prayer and faith in God? There are no limitations in life. There are no constraints except the ones self-imposed. The Bible says as a man thinks in his heart so is he (Proverbs 23:7).

Jesus said, "Have faith in God. Whosoever shall say to the mountain, be removed, and be cast into the sea; and shall not doubt in his heart, but shall believe what he says, that person will have whatsoever he says" (Mark 11:23). The key words are *have faith in God*. No matter how much gold is found *in them there hills,* life apart from the one who makes gold is profitless. The only limitation in life would be to live in a world separated from the source of life. The understanding of sin is understood not just as that which is bad, but as that which separates the human child from his heavenly Father—God.

Chapter 8
The Way of All the Earth

This chapter's title phrase is mentioned several places in the Bible. It refers to the general design of the cosmos, set it motion by God. Some of the basic principles follow:

Seed time and Harvest & Sowing and Reaping

This principle declares that for every planting or sowing there will yield a harvest of that which was planted or sowed. This is also called the Law of Genesis. In Genesis, the first book of the Bible, everything was produced after its own kind. If it were a bird, it produced more birds, not more fish. If it were a horse, it produced another horse, not a monkey. If it were an apple, it produced an apple tree and more apples, not a cherry tree or a persimmon.

Likewise, man was designed to (and called to) produce after his own kind. This is where the word mankind originates. Man's offspring were more men, not giraffes, elephants or tomatoes. Man is the only creature that was produced in the image and likeness of God. Although the balance of creation was designed by God, man came from the very seed of God.

God created everything by speaking it into existence. The Bible and the Book of Genesis is full of what and how God said. The conclusion of God's words in creation was His words in acceptance of what He created. He would create by saying, "Let there be." He would conclude by saying, "It is good and very good." Man was also to speak and order his world the same way. Man, however, is not the creator but the child of the creator. Mankind's authority does not come from men speaking their own original words but speaking and adhering to the words of his Father.

When the flood of Noah's day came, God promised the survivors of the flood (Noah and his family and all the animals in Genesis 8) that there would be no more worldwide flood of water. He also said in verse 22, "While the earth remains, there would be seedtime and harvest, and cold and heat, and summer and winter, and day and night shall not cease." God was declaring at that time that the principles for establishing your future would still be intact.

The Bible says that the power of life and death is in the tongue or mouth—our words (Proverbs 18:21). God says those that love and live by this very principle would eat its fruit, which is the result of what they've been speaking. If you understand that your destiny is governed by what you say and what you do you would live by the words of your mouth. Again, the Bible is clear where the power of your own words have value. The true power of affecting your destiny and future comes from being a son or daughter of God (one who has a real relationship with Him). The power to have the fruits and rewards of a magnificent fulfilling future is speaking God's Word. God's Word will never contradict. His Word will never support evil or anything that does not bring glory to Him.

The Life Cycle
The Experience of Life

After the duration of natural life, man (kind) must return his flesh (body) back to the ground. Actually, this applies to all creation. This denotes an exchange and interchange of all creation with itself. The only difference is that man, in one sense, is symbiotic. He is a spirit being living in an animal-type body. Man is a spirit, possessing a soul and lives in a body. (To note: some interpret the spirit and the soul as being the same. However the same conclusion is reached) The Bible in Genesis 2:7 says God breathed breath or spirit into man's body and man became a living soul (paraphrased). However, by no confusion, the man and his flesh are one being on the earth. The reference implies only that man has an extraterrestrial element to his nature. A man's body is essentially his earth suit. This earth suit is also man's license of authority on this planet. In this suit, man has dominion on the earth. It is from where his body was created and the earth was made for his habitation, domain and rule. However, if the flesh body were to die, it must return to where it came from, ashes to ashes and dust to dust; returned since the day it grew from a tiny cell in the depths of a woman's womb; returned since the day its body was infused with breath from God the creator. So by these truths, the general outcome of all beings could be predicted; unless, there was perhaps some external or divine phenomenon that would interrupt.

Some people approach a proclaimed fortuneteller or fortune telling device with the hope that the forecast doesn't hold early and pending tales of doom or death. Even shadowed in the word of an expected promise is the question of how long will the manifestation last? In the finiteness of our human minds, it is hard to mentally frame the picture of eternity. In the earth realm we live, it is hard to comprehend the reality of eternity—a place that never, ever runs out. Even the little bunny with the battery and drums is perceived to run out eventually if the commercial lingered. The cut flowers brought home and given to a loved one, though beautiful, in reality have already died. The Thanksgiving meal that took hours to make is gone in twenty minutes or less. The feast is over, the relatives go home, and then back to work on Friday or Monday. The saying, nothing lasts forever has long been accepted.

We cherish memories. Memories are painting of things in the life cycle that have been experienced. The memory of that first long-awaited kiss (from your husband or wife) will last sometimes for years. Even when it has faded into the sunset of memories gone by, it can still be remembered by pictures, old letters, reflection or conversation. Truly, without an experience there is no true memory. A memory for which there is no experience is called a *Fantasy*. Fantasy can never satisfy. An experience that produced a memory is always better and longer lasting than a fantasy.

Again, looking at life through the eyes of eternity can be challenging. Sometimes memories of things that have already been experienced can be fleeting. Yet so much of the perception of the future is based on memories of things that have past. To envision a life that never ends, and flourishes even beyond death, is doubly challenging. Again, it is based on the point of reference. To embrace eternity, and living life in it, requires a revelation greater than a memory or a fantasy.

Someone described eternity as a dream that we never wake from. Perhaps we should view the present as the dream. It is true that the duration of the present compared to eternity is as a dream. However, the present is just as real as eternity. Interestingly, what we do in the present affects our place in eternity.

Experiencing eternity is not founded in a memory, dream or a fantasy. It is not found in the precognition of an event. Life and eternity are rooted in a *Promise*. A promise is a declaration based on the words of another and the ability of that one to carry out that promise. It is also the commitment of the one making the promise to bring it to pass.

Let's say God were to make a promise to us. We would base the fulfilling of that promise on God's integrity and past history. Perhaps God, in order to convince us, could swear to us that His promise is true. Usually, for a human to swear to the utmost, he would swear by God or take an oath upon a Bible, or upon some object, person, or creed. The person swearing would have to swear by something greater than himself. This swearing would be the testimonial that the truth that was just told is as true, or as sure, as that which it was sworn on. Simplified, if the object of the swearing would fail, so would the truth or promise. If God were to swear, He would have to swear by Himself or upon Himself (because there is nothing greater than God) to confirm the promise He made. This would affirm that if the promise made by God would fail, so would God Himself. If God were to fail, it would be self-destruction to Him and all that He created.

But what would God have to give as a track record? If the promise He made was for eternity (or eternal life) how could we trust Him? In His deposition, God would have to have given an infallible proof of His promise, truth and commitment. He would have to show where He, in fact, was tested. And it would have to be a test that in deed cost Him all. In other words, God would have to reveal something that would prove that His Word was good.

The fullness of this type of commitment would have to be shown in death or martyrdom. But if God were dead who would run creation while He was dead. But if He could somehow give Himself to death and still exist as God, then maybe. But then of course, He is God. If He could do that, then His promises could be accepted infallible as truth. Then we could put all trust in whatever He said, even His promise of life and eternal life. If we visit the book of truth (the Bible) again and find several places (Hebrews 6:13-19 and John 3:16) we will find that He did that very thing.

Based on this premise, if God would do that, then everything else He said would be true, including His claims about eternal life. There was a man named Abraham who believed God, and obeyed God, to the altering of the future. He believed God's promises would ascend beyond the point of death. God would fulfill His promise even if He had to resurrect the dead. I have found that it is upon these promises that my eternity and the longevity of my life rest. There is a promise that God made in the Bible in Psalm 103:1-5:

Bless the LORD, O my soul: and all that is within me, bless his holy name. [2] Bless the LORD, O my soul, and forget not all his benefits: [3] Who forgiveth all thine iniquities; who healeth all thy diseases; [4] who redeemeth thy life from destruction; who crowneth thee with lovingkindness and tender mercies; [5] who satisfieth thy mouth with good things; so that thy youth is renewed like the eagle's.

Another Scripture says:
"With Long Life will He satisfy me and show me His salvation." Psalm 91:16

And Again:
[11] **Thou wilt shew me the path of life**: *in thy presence is fullness of joy; at thy right hand there are* **pleasures for evermore**. *Psalms 16:11*

This becomes the source of tomorrow, not some glance into the future. It is a glance into the future, but it's a glance to live by.

The Course of Nature

One definition of this biblical phrase that expresses *The Course of Nature* is the wheel of human origin, which as soon as men are born begins to run its course of life—genesis. As soon as a child is born (or as another biblical phrase explains, "breaks the matrix,") it has set in motion a chain of events that undoubtedly will happen. The course of life begins not when the child breaks through the door of vaginal cleft (the door is another biblical term), but when conception has occurred. I know there may be a lot of groans to those who read this book from a prochoice viewpoint, but to believe in future prediction of any kind, the wonderful mystery of conception, the marriage of male and female DNA, has to be believed as the fulfilling of human destiny.

It was the prophet Jeremiah who said God chose him when he was still in his mother's womb. It was the Apostle Paul who said he was chosen to ministry before the cosmos were created. Of course this is a reality that needs to be faced. If destiny can lay dormant in the fertilized egg of a woman, then how many potential world-changers have not been allowed? Abortion is not only applicable to the fetus but to a course of life, a path in human destiny that was a not allowed or aborted. The mother is then only the host. The womb becomes the porthole for which children of destiny may enter the earth. The mother becomes host and nurturer of possible world-changers.

We begin to entertain all the sociological and psychological terms such as nurture and nature. Is a child a product of his biological disposition or his environment? A *baby* is a product of a male and female incorporated via a biological act. A *child* is a product of those who input into his life. A child's nature is representative of his father. Someone will father a child, whether that father be of biological, sociological or spiritual composition. Someone will input into the child.

A child is born to characterize the nature of his father. This father-child relationship is not just by birth, it is by identification, acceptance and obedience. According to the Bible a child who refuses to adhere to the discipline of his father is a bastard. The reason why (author's perspective) children tend to emulate their natural father may not have to do with genetics. The linkage may be more attached to a course of nature that was set into motion by words that were spoken and believed in the life of the biological mother & father (and their mother & father). It's not life in the ghetto or Wall Street that spawn character, but the words that are spoken and believed that will develop a child of any environment. Ghetto mentality can live in those we call rich. Wealthy mentality can live in those who live in the ghetto. However, if it is allowed to blossom and grow, an innovative wealthy disposition will pull a man out of the ghetto. Accordingly, a ghetto mentality will pull a man into the ghetto. He may live in the big house on the hill but live in a dark alley inside his heart.

I stated earlier that the child conceived or received has set in motion a chain of events called the course of life. The child has also entered a chain of events. He has entered into a world that is governed by physical and spiritual laws. Regardless of what is spoken and believed, and unless there is divine intervention, the child will have to experience these laws and their effects. These include things like birth itself, breath, some hurt, some pain, death, and hopefully—great expectation of happiness and love.

The biblical phrase is found in the book of James 3:6 and the association is not with a set trail of events. That which causes this wheel of life and destiny to turn is the power of words. It says the words that people speak determine their destiny. It also declares that the forces of Hell, if allowed, can offer the tongue a course and pattern to live. The forces of Hell are all those forces that will cause a man to live in a hellish state on earth and live through eternity in Hell at the end cycle of his human existence.

The word zodiac refers to a circle or band. It refers to the constellations which fall in a set circular pattern, respective to the orbit of the earth, moon, and other planets. Some fortune tellers and horoscope writers base their knowledge on the zodiac. The horoscope gives words to the tongues of its readers. The future wheel is then set in motion by those who embrace, speak and believe what they heard and read.

James 3:3-6 KJV

Behold, we put bits in the horses' mouths, that they may obey us; and we turn about their whole body.[4] Behold also the ships, which though they be so great, and are driven of fierce winds, yet are they turned about with a very small helm, whithersoever the governor listeth.⁵ Even so the tongue is a little member, and boasteth great things. Behold, how great a matter a little fire kindleth!⁶ And the tongue is a fire, a world of iniquity: so is the tongue among our members, that it defileth the whole body, and setteth on fire the course of nature; and it is set on fire of hell.

James 3: 6 Amplified Bible
⁶And the tongue is a fire. [The tongue is a] world of wickedness set among our members, contaminating and depraving the whole body and setting on fire the wheel of birth (the cycle of man's nature), being itself ignited by hell (Gehenna).

Chapter 9
Can the Future Really Be Known?

The theme of this book is—*How to Predict the Future*. This is a statement of my intent as the author and not a posed question. The question of the book or its premise is the topic of this chapter; can the future really be known? We have presented arguments and positions, but can it really be known? Does this book have truth or relevance (another question)? Or, is it just fanciful thoughts and ideas. All in all, it may come to point of view. The individuals who may challenge are God (and He's has the final word), the author, the reader, and any person who attest to the ability to predict. Before the concepts of future predictions can be validated, the concept of the future must be understood. Is the future an inalterable pre-destiny or is it an upcoming event that is affected by a continual chain of decisions? If the future can be changed, the claims of future telling and other soothsaying would be only warnings.

When a flower seed is planted in the ground, one can predict the seed will manifest whatever the picture on the seed package depicts. However, it would take a special intuitive ability (or a doctorate in genetics) to predict that a seed identical to another (in the same package) would produce a different color flower. There are other scenarios that would affect the future of the flower. The plant could be pruned in a way that only a chosen number of flowers would grow on it. In this scenario, the plant itself would have been altered by manipulation, but the color of the flowers may be still the same. And of course one could always dye the flowers regardless of what the genetic outcome produced.

A seed contains within itself everything that will make the seed what it will become. Its very master plan is stored. However, if purposely manipulated, abused, guided, weighed down, pruned, altered or somehow affected at its roots, the future of the seed will have been changed. This change from what it was designed to be could be positive. Water and the right sunlight can positively affect it. Plant food and good soil nutrition can positively affect it.

The difference between the plant and a human is that the plant does not have free-will or choice. A human child may not have been able to choose the family or the environment it was born in, but it does have the ability to choose where its life ends up, no matter how challenging that choice may be. The success of a flower's growth is because its entire clothing and covering, springs out from within. Its future is not external but internal. Although it still has an ultimate future, the flower can't choose its future. Humans have a choice in producing their daily and ultimate future.

How does this describe human future? The seed of the plant contains the order of life that has predestined what the plant and the flower would become. Still, the distinct outcome or future can be changed or ordered. Future prediction then is not a revelation of known pre-events. It is the understanding of the possessed ability to choose and change individual future and destiny.

It appears that cause and effect play a major part in future prediction. Although preprogrammed, the future can be altered. However, the ultimate future, in the scenario of the plant, would be still inevitable; that is, it would eventually perish or change in existence. Often what is a future prediction entertains only the timeline of events, which can be altered. The ultimate eternity and the core existence of the time, generation, person, place or thing are left ignored. In other words, fortune telling only deals with timelines, whether past or present. Fortune telling has little to do with understanding eternity.

The knowledge of a person's future (or past) is not the cure to anxiety. It is not necessarily the basis for decision making. What is more revelatory is a person's ability to alter, change and affect his future. It is also the person's ability to discern and make choices. It's a person's ability to be free from mental and emotional bondage, which affect making right decisions. The Bible declares the power of life and death is in a person's tongue (Proverbs 18:21), that is, in the words he speaks or his ability to choose his own destiny.

So if a person has the ability to affect his future, how can soothsaying be the ultimate prediction? Decision and outcome could be determined by simple investigation of choices and the outcome they would produce. However, if we look at the future, where timelines are concerned, one can predict the future based on knowing what decision an individual (or his generation) has made or will make.

If words and choices can change a person's future and destiny, then fortune telling and horoscopes only present words and choices to be accepted and believed. The believer (not the medium) has become the teller of his own future. If there is another force manipulating the predictions of the fortuneteller, the fortuneteller becomes the pawn. The person whose fortune is being told is a pawn twice moved. In other words, the individual would believe what was said, and then manipulate his destiny by simply believing and embracing what was said.

I must disclose that not all preachers of future choosing agree. Some philosophies believe in *Predestination.* This is the belief that where a person's eternal destiny is concerned, men do not have free will to choose. In this belief system, man's ultimate destiny and eternity has been predetermined by God and cannot be altered. This belief borders another belief called *Fate* (next chapter).

Chapter 10
Prophetic Destiny

The term "prophetic destiny" is used in some Christian circles. It is the term referring to an assignment given to individuals from God, even before they were in their mother's womb. God told the prophet Jeremiah that he had been called to be a prophet before his infant eyes had ever seen the outside world (Jeremiah 1:5). Paul the apostle said a person's life could be ordered before the world was even made (Ephesians 1:4). There is a belief that all of mankind, every individual, has that same prophetic call. There is a path laid by God for every person to walk. As stated in an earlier chapter, there is a God ordained purpose for everyone to fulfill.

The fulfilling of this prophetic destiny is not necessarily definite. It is assuredly definite on the side of God Almighty. But the individual for whom prepared may have some say in the fulfilling of his course. The Bible says a fool could die before his time (Ecclesiastes 7:17). The book of Proverbs (Chapter 7) illustrates a young man in route to somewhere, but he is enticed into an adulterous act after being seduced. He was on the course, but never reached his original destination. Because of temptation, he was drawn off course by his own choices. The book of 1 Kings (Chapter 13) speaks of a prophet who had an assignment from God but was lead off track and was killed. He was killed because he was redirected by the words of another prophet of God. The other prophet lied to the one who received the instructions. The lying prophet professed to speak in the name of the Lord, because he wanted the first prophet to visit with him.

Prophetic destiny is different from fate. Fate is a preset destiny that cannot be altered. A person's fate is the point that individual ends up at in the walk of life. The path can be altered, but the final destination is always the same. It would also mean any point on the path, if viewed as the destination for that time period, would have been inalterable. In other words, the clothes you have on right now, the place you are reading this book, the last meal you ate were inalterably destined to happen, even if you had worn something else or ate a different meal. If it sounds confusing—it is.

Religious philosophies and doctrines have emanated from these ideas. The term "fatalism" declares that a person's actions, state in life or future may not necessarily be based on the individual's free will, but on the will of a supreme being, a governing force or fate itself. This also draws the conclusion that there are no mistakes in life. There are no human manifested plunders or blunders. Wars are inevitable. So are sicknesses, plagues, accidents and strangers meeting in the night. It is all the result of fate or divine will.

Divine will does have its rights and place in the outcome of humanity as a whole and the steering of all humanity to its ultimate destiny. However, we will find the individual's fate in life and the divine influence may be directly related to accepted invitations (allowing God to move), choices and prayer. The exception would be the calling of God for a person's life. God Himself would woo a person into a calling (a distinct plan), but the person would still have to choose and accept the plan. Usually, this would be a plan ultimately affecting the steering of humanity or a group of humanity to its ultimate destiny. So said, God Almighty has the final word.

Chapter 11
Peace of Mind

I know the thoughts that I think toward you – to give you an expected end (future) Jeremiah 29:11 (KJV). For I know the thoughts that I think toward you, says the LORD, thoughts of peace and not of evil, to give you a future and a hope (NKJV).

The Bible declares that real peace is not just in knowing the future, but in knowing it has been founded in peace and filled with hope. The writer says having someone who keeps your success and welfare continually on his mind is a good thing. A future of hope is solid when we know we have someone who is definitely on our side and for us.

I have heard people say, "I don't need anybody. I am self-sufficient. I am self-confident. I can make it on my own in life. I don't need any aid or support from any one."

It is good to be self-sufficient and posses all the characteristics of a survivor in a world that can sometimes be a merciless jungle. However, the reality still surfaces, and the human psyche cannot survive for long without companionship. There is an internal design that demands fellowship with like beings. In this passage, the writer's peace rests (in the revelation) that his future security is a continual thought on the mind of God

Almighty. God's thoughts and hand (His goodness) on our future is the ultimate comfort.

Sometimes the human psyche itself tries to bring peace on its own. On the positive side, this can be found in some entertainment or vacation. The mind will draw upon pleasant memories stored. Unhappiness and pain, from the mind mending its own, can be the withdrawal that comes from depression. The mind finds a hiding place within itself. The brain answers with chemical shifts and imbalances to compensate. If the result continues untreated, depression can be serious and deadly. Man was not designed to cope with life based on his own found resources. Man was called to win in life. God gave man the resources in life to win. The Bible says that a man's spirit (Proverbs 18:14) will bear his infirmities (sickness, weakness, and hurts). It also says in that same passage, "but a wounded spirit who can bear." The spirit of man is to be his resource but not his source. A resource is the means or the door for attaining. A source is the provider to the resource. The infamous analogy again asks, "is the glass half full or half empty?" The pessimist says half empty and the happy-go-lucky optimist says half full. The realist says, "Just show me the pitcher, faucet, fountain or well." The reality says, whether half-empty or half-full, it will have to be filled at sometime. I want to know the source. God, who is life itself, is the source. He is the healer of depression, and restorer from oppression, and all else related. True peace of mind comes from God, not the mind trying to be God.

Studies show that people who have foundations in an organized religion system, such as a church, have an easier time coming out of depression. Conversely, lurking in the shadows of depression may be sorrow over broken commitments to God. However, the redemptive light is that forgiveness comes from God. Having a faith in God and having the support system from a church family has been found to be important in faster recovery from depression.

Although salvation from God is true, please note the references in this book are not rooted in religion but in a relationship with the living God. Some have said that if you are a Christian you are immature and need a crutch. If that statement was meant to be a question in disguise the answer is a resounding "yes." Just as the human body needs the support of its skeleton to cause it to stand erect under the force of gravity, so does every man need the reassurance, support and help of the Creator and Savior. This is the peace of the future. An old spiritual song says, "He (God) has the whole world in His hand".

The future cannot be escaped. Death or suicide could never provide escape. The pressure of the present shouts an eternity. The strength of depression is the thought of being oppressed forever. Escape is never found in death; it is only found in life. Life is where choices are made. When the choice is for the life that God gives, peace becomes the reality and the expectation.

Chapter 12
How Does Fortune Telling Work?

There are several shows on TV that depict how a crime was committed. Often the discoveries are rather detailed. Sometimes the crime was committed years and decades before. The science of forensic medicine together with detective work has long been used but has become more popular to the public in recent years. Forensic medicine follows a trail of evidence. Sometimes this evidence is so minuscule to the untrained that when discovered, it appears to be a wonder or magic to the onlooker. However, to the expert a clear trail or line becomes clearer and clearer to his watchful senses. We discover that tangible things like science aid in knowing the mysteries of past and future.

The use of DNA to resolve crimes or any unanswered mystery has become commonplace. A person's whole genetic makeup and identity can be found in a trace of blood or in a strand of hair. Once the identity can be established, other pieces of the story can be fit together so that the story then begins to unfold. Sometimes the picture is cloudy, but if it is delved into enough, it will produce a readable image.

I saw a movie once where Sherlock Holmes walked into Sigmund Freud's office and was able to tell his whole life story by observing the pictures on the wall and other things in the room including the man himself. As an example, I could discern or predict that the reader of this book has some interest in knowing his future. I surmise by the simple fact that you are reading (or listening to) this book on predicting the future. I could further predict that you have thought about having your future told. I could also presume that you have had once or twice experimented in this area but wanted to know more. You are probably a shy person with a lot of questions; you are probably not quick to share your thoughts with other people. If that line of study was not true I could probably detour off and follow another list of assumptions, all because you are reading this book. I could further deduce that you are a curious individual who likes knowledge of a variety of subjects. Perhaps you are over a friend's house and noticed this book lying on her (or his) dining room table.

In other words, the world is full of clues that are screaming out to us, talking to us, trying to reveal something to us. The understanding is in knowing how to read them. There is always a definite path, a definite course of study. Either it's our plan or we have been taken along on a ride of someone else's plan. Everything has an answer. The key is in knowing the secret. Sometimes like the TV game show *Jeopardy* the answer is given and you must give the right question. I submit to you that for most things in this life, the answers have been given. You must know the right questions. Many of life's mysteries undoubtedly fall into several categories.

- Illusion (whether by sleight of hand or by a device of some kind)
- Mental illusion, such as with hypnosis or suggestion
- Nature & Science
- Asleep at the wheel
- Demonic influence
- Divine influence

Illusion

If you ever had a magician come to a birthday party when you were a child or saw an infamous TV illusionist make an airplane disappear, you were exposed to illusion. Illusionists have used from centuries past a plethora of techniques to present their craft. There have been techniques that use mirrors to reflect images into fog or mist and elaborate boxes with trap doors and secret compartments to make people disappear. These events seemingly defy the laws of nature. Even the uncle that always tries to impress his nieces and nephews by pulling a quarter out of their ear is a demonstration of illusion or sleight of hand. The illusionist's art is to perform the stunt without having his onlookers see how he did it. (It would probably be more impressive for the uncle just to give his nephew or niece ten bucks right into their hands.)

As I was speaking of the boardwalk earlier in this book, among the crowds there was always a performer on the side, entertaining. Many of these entertainers were street magicians or casino-hired magicians entertaining the travelers. Some were using the crowd to perfect their art. Everyone in the crowd watched with the idea that he could figure out how the trick was performed. Often the answer was obvious; sometimes overanalyzing things can lead to being misled or tricked. For example, the magician throwing specks of light to his partner is amazing. We try to focus on the light. We think how many there are, and how fast they are being tossed. The reality may be that they are simply flickering lights held by both the performer and his partner. Now, this is not to minimize any good magician's act. Many have spent years practicing their craft. Even though we somehow know it's a trick, we applaud the talent that will fool us the best. *Walt Disney World* has done the same thing with its theme parks. The magic that is portrayed by animators on the screen is recreated by technology at the parks. The result is the same; we leave each event wowed and amazed although we know it was an illusion.

The association of magic with the magician is probably not accurate. Parlor magicians used sleight of hand, science, tricks or illusion. The first definition of magic would be more associated with witchcraft. This definition is invoking charms and potions to control the forces of nature and to interfere in the lives of people. The alignment between the two definitions is the focus on another person, other than God Almighty, to impress and alter the input and outcomes of life.

Mental illusion & Hypnosis

There are subtle forms of illusions such as *mental illusion, hypnosis* or suggestion. The advertising market has used these devices for year. There were questions of ethics years ago about the use of subliminal message in movies. An advertiser could insert a clip of film into a movie that was so fast that the human eye could not perceive the image. The subconscious, which supposedly captures everything, would record the image. Since the conscious mind could not see the image or suggestion, it could not reason against it. The result is that the subconscious would try to act the suggestion out. If a split second frame flashed the words, "I'm thirsty," then the body, as directed by the subconscious, would begin to desire something to drink—preferably something expensive behind the counter at the concession stand.

Whether ethical or not, advertisers have been hiding other images in their visual ads for years. These images impress the subconscious mind with certain human desires, like sex. Again since the subconscious mind could not rationalize, the mind and memory would associate the strong human desires with the item that was for sale.

Nature & Science

Nature itself has long seduced us. How many tribal rituals were sanctified by the eclipse of the moon or sun? A rainbow in its simplicity still amazes me. How each one of trillions of snowflakes can all be different amazes me. How the sky is blue because of refraction and reflection of light is a wonder. I know the colorful sunrise and sunset is caused by the angle of the light coming through the atmosphere, but it is still beautiful to me every morning and night.

Science is probably one the greatest uses of illusion. If we captured mystical (or sublime) events of nature and then caused them to be repeated over and over at will, we call it an invention. These inventions have lighted homes and cities. These inventions have sent men to the moon and back. These inventions have aided in the cure of diseases and have increased the harvest of farmers. These inventions have made the world a lot smaller. There is the reality that my friend can live thousands of miles across the ocean, but the illusion caused by a telephone and now the Internet has put my friend at the table with me.

Asleep at the Wheel

Sometimes just *being asleep*, missing the punch line or the ending of a movie, can cause the illusion. I thought this in high school algebra II class. I would sometimes follow the formula at the beginning but sometimes seemed to miss something in between. It was the "in between" that resulted in the answer or the solution.

I remember my father who would work hard all day and then go out to church meetings at night. Sometimes he would be so tired that we'd find him in the car asleep with the car still running. He would not remember how he got home in the driveway. Sometimes life will pull these sleeper moments, such as not knowing when trouble or an event had crept into our lives. It may have been because we were sleep at the wheel. Sometimes we can focus on distractions around us and not focus on the real deal in our lives.

Demonic Influence

We talked about this in the sections on familiar spirits. Sometimes a soothsayer, palm reader, or witch will often engage the use of a demonic spirit to assist them. This method may or may not be known by the user but it still produces the same results. We must understand that this world we live in is not physical only. We live in a world that is inhabited by spirits. These are beings we can't see. Some of these beings, such as God, His Holy Spirit, and His angels work together for the good of those who love God. Other beings, such as demonic sprits, have a different mission. Their purpose is to willfully deceive. Their influence is to affect the future of the individuals on earth so that they lose focus on their ultimate future. They would rather have people focus on short-term temporal events. Temporal events are subject to choices made in life not by prediction. Sometime it's just a fifty-fifty proposition, but a different choice will always affect the outcome of things or the way things outcome.

Sometimes the talk of other spirits inhabiting the world next to us can be unsettling, but not to worry because human beings themselves, you and I, are also spirits. The only differences are that we live in a body and can encounter, experience and make choices in this corporal world. According to the Bible, under God, human beings have the decision-making authority in this world. Man has the direct say in what is allowed and what is not allowed on the earth. It's not God or the devil that causes wars. It's men who either choose to listen to God or to the devil. Even

God came to earth as a man to affect human history. Jesus completed His assignment to the cross. He then commissioned His followers (speaking embodied spirits) in His name to carry out His plan and preach His gospel.

Divine Influence

Again, this is not supposed to be a religious book, but the references to God, Jesus and the Bible are necessary to tell the truth concerning *future telling*. Many times subjects like this leave the *Divine influence* out. One can't have true science or true study of any kind without the Divine influence. One can't be atheistic or agnostic about this. Without the Divine there is not even the hope of any kind of *future*. We must understand that the concept of hope, which is synonymous with future, is not of human creation; it is implanted by the Divine God Almighty Himself.

God has intervened in the affairs of men with Himself. When this is understood, the finite of the everyday is swallowed by infinity. The boardwalk in Atlantic City supplies a different joy for me than the casinos. It is a place to view the ocean. When I view the vastness of the ocean and compare it to any personal conflicts, the ocean swallows up the conflicts. When I gaze into the horizon where the ocean and sky meet, I realize God made the sea. The ocean along with my conflicts is swallowed up by God. When I gaze into the vastness of God I remember that He is the creator of all, including me. At that time, when I remember and realize His vast love for me, I am swallowed up in Him.

To everything there is a season, and a time to every purpose under the heaven:

Ecclesiastes 3:1

Chapter 13
Psychic Phenomenon

Let's take a moment to talk about this subject because there are so many things that are categorized under the title of Psychic Phenomenon. Everything from *ESP*, dreams, some religious practices, ghosts, poltergeists and even extraterrestrial encounters are included.

Usually psychic phenomena are compared to that hazy unexplained *deja vu* realm of occurrence, events for which there is no known explanation. Another word would be p*aranormal*. The prefix *para* means outside or beyond and the root word *normal* meaning that which is part of the routine chain of events. The paranormal occurrence is an (usually unexplained) event outside and beyond the routine chain of events. The cult TV show *The Twilight Zone* (1959-64, 1985-89, and 2002-03) dealt with this subject.

We as humans love to explain every event in our lives and in this world. Doing so allows a sense of control and stability. Human beings are uncomfortable in situations where there is no control or where things are unexplained. However, there is still the fascination with the things that are beyond the normal realm. This fascination springs from a desire to believe that we are not limited to the here and now. These concepts and fantasies are not necessarily rational to the brain or the subconscious.

They are thoughts that emanate from the design of the universe itself. This is the design in which we are a part. There are forces outside of what we perceive with the natural senses. However, these forces are not as mystical as we would think.

Everything in the universe is governed by laws. Because a law hasn't been formulated or grasped does not disprove its existence or nullify its effects. Two of those are the laws of *sowing and reaping* and *covenant allegiances*. I will not discuss these in detail in this book, but see the section on seedtime and harvest. Everything that happens has been designed and is a product of something else. When we can understand this we can understand the most unexplained occurrences and the strangest phenomena.

Beyond the Senses

Man has been endowed with five predominate senses. These senses help us to communicate, explore, exist and prosper in a material world. The problem is that the existence of other presences, realms and incorporeal beings seem to share time and space with us. Different unexplained encounters suggest an intangible world existing on the same plane and geography as the tangible. Just the thought of the existence of this other world gives claim to the ability of some to sense its movements. Some suggest that some or perhaps all humans (and animals) have additional senses that allow interaction with this world. Those additional senses or a six sense are categorized (in this book) as *Intuition*, *Premonitions*, *Discernment*, *Forewarning* and *Animal Senses*. This supernatural sensing does not always claim the existence of a living active inhabited world within ours, but suggest an extra cognitive dimension beyond the normal that allow insight into the future of our own.

The definitions of these topics are usually based on interpretation. Sometimes they are defined by hindsight and followed by the expression "Oh, that's what that meant." There is a collection of old wives' tales. An old wives' tale is superstitious folklore, a story based on an unexplained phenomenon, explained and categorized with something tangible. Every culture and world region no doubt has its own scrapbooks of these ideas.

The term *sixth sense* is often thought of in relationship to psychic phenomena. The 1999 Hollywood movie *The Six Sense* portrayed it as the ability to talk to the spirits of the dead. Using that concept, the sixth sense is the ability to perceive what others can't through the five physical senses. It is through the five physical senses of taste, touch, sight, hearing, and feeling that a normal person contacts and perceives the carnal (corporal) world. Those with the ability to sense something that the five senses can't, would be thought to have this sixth sense. Of course, this would also mean in order to perceive something through a sixth sense there would have to be something outside the *five sense* world to perceive.

Intuition is different. A person who moves by intuition or "a knowing" also perceives the world differently than others who may live by the carnal (natural) senses. However, intuition is more of the ability to interpret the outside world based on an internal, unlearned cognition or inner voice.

A *premonition* is an event that happens before another event but is interpreted as a sign or forewarning that danger may be approaching. Often the tools for interpretation are based on passed down tales. Superstition can have an affect on interpreting premonitions. A black cat that crosses the path, a broken mirror, or an overturned cup of tea are examples. A premonition may also be a dream, thought or feeling that appears to be some forewarning.

Animals are often said to have the ability to perceive or see things that the human eye can't. The dog that stops in its tracks, the cat whose back fur sticks straight up, the bug that cringes or speeds away even before you raise your hand to squash it—as if it perceived that you were about to impact its future. *Animals* can often *sense* a storm arising before the sky darkening. Hordes of animals in the jungle begin to run in terror days before an earthquake or volcanic eruption take places. It may be an inner ear placed (by God) inside of these beings we often call dumb animals. Interestingly, it was only the animals that along with Noah's family entered the ark before the great flood.

All these things relate to how the five-sense world is perceived. It also dictates how the carnal world may be speaking. It may be surprising to understand the voices (not mystical) that the natural world is really giving off. It also speaks of a governing of the physical world by supernatural force. Scripture says God is upholding the world by the Word of His power (Hebrew 1:3). There is a scripture that says the whole creation groans in expectation waiting for manifestation of the sons of God (Romans 8:19-23). One interpretation of this scripture suggest that the natural world whether inanimate (as with rock or vegetation) or animate (as with animals) literally sighs in waiting for God's offspring to positively affect the earth.

The term *discernment* is also a foreknowing or perceiving. The simplest definition of discernment is the voice of wisdom interpreting and seeing through a situation, person or event in the perceived world. In the truest definition, it is the voice of God revealing and exposing real intentions. It is also God revealing unseen supernatural forces in operation, forces that affect the lives of individuals, families, regions, and nations. *Biblical discernment* is a gift from God and does not reflect some idolized gift of an individual. Biblical discernment reflects willingness from God to help His people. Discernment is not just a revelation of something bad, but a revelation of the operation of God and His host at work.

[9]*But now that you know God—or rather are known by God—how is it that you are turning back to those weak and miserable principles? Do you wish to be enslaved by them all over again?* [10]*You are observing special days and months and seasons and years!* [11]*I fear for you, that somehow I have wasted my efforts on you.*
Galatians 4:9,10 NIV Bible

Chapter 14
Is the Future the Final Destiny?

The Bible speaks of events that will take place in the future. These events are like water in a cup, swelling at the brim, but have not yet run over. The Bible takes us to a place in time where there is God sitting on the throne judging the dead—great and small. The Biblical prophet who penned the book of Revelation says after this he saw a new Heaven and a new Earth, for the old Heaven and Earth were passed away. In the atmospheric heaven there was no more sun or moon. On the earth there were no more oceans or seas. This revelation of a different world is not unique to the earth and sky but its greatest claim is concerning its inhabitants. The Bible proclaims that in this new creation or re-creation corporeal life will go on forever. This is called eternal life.

We can call *eternity* the future as relative to now, but in reality there is no time there. It is often hard to imagine these things in the finite capacity of our minds. Our ability to reason is based on information that we know and have learned. We are accustomed to a world that exists within four-dimensions: height, width, length and time. If we can think outside this box for at least one moment and imagine what God has spoken and promised, we would see a glimpse of the wonders that He has in store. It is written in Corinthians 2:9 *Eye has not seen, nor ear heard, neither has entered into the heart of man, the things which God has prepared for them that love Him. But God has revealed them by His spirit: for the Spirit searches all things, yea, the deep things of God.*

In the series of movies called *Final Destination* (premiering in 2000) the characters who avoided death meet horrible demises throughout the plot of the movie. The movie works with the premise that death is the final destination of humanity (and its individuals) that ultimately cannot be escaped. The script speaks either it's now or later.

I was delivering newspapers, in the early morning hours of August 31—1997, when the news of *Princess Diana* death headlined. As an earlier morning news deliverer (and on the east coast) I was one of the first to receive the news before the rest of the world (at least in the western nations). I'll never forget, out of all the news releases of celebrities who died, this one seemed to grip me more. I believe it may have been my perception of her life, as one so young and promising. She was a living fairy tale. The paparazzi and tabloids made her life so tangible to many. Unfortunately, her magical life was early ended.

I remember the scripture that surface in me (Revelations 12:12-15). In the midst of the grief—I saw the dead great and small standing before God's throne. Suddenly it did not matter who she was in this life. It no longer mattered on earth the relevancy of the tiara the Princess wore. It only now mattered what her relationship was with the King of kings who sat on the throne of heaven and eternity. Celebrities of all stature die every day, but all around the earth, so do those who are unrenowned. When I hear of someone who departed the earth in death my first response is, "Where did they go?"

Death is not the final destination. I'll state without allowing the argument—knowing that the atheist and agnostic disagree. Heaven and Hell share at least one common doctrinal commonality; there are no atheists or agnostics in either place. One day, on a job that I worked, two spiritually irreverent men were having fun joking—being sarcastic about God and spiritual things. Being in the same room and undoubtedly offended, the Holy Spirit impressed in me a holy enigma. I immediately blurted it out to the men. "What's the difference between heaven and hell?" It silenced their foolishness and grabbed their attention. They answered quickly that they did not know. Quickly prompted by the same unknown unction, I blurted the answer, "You!"

The whole concept of a door speaks to having an *in* and an *out*. Doors don't open to a wall. Doors open to a different place. However death is not the door to eternity. It is a way of passage. The door to eternity is a person. His name is Jesus Christ. Walking through that door is by choice. The final destination of a human being is to make a choice at that door. If a person does not choose to enter that door, he still will meet eternity; but it will not be the glorious one that God has destined and prepared.

The Revelation of Jesus Christ, which God gave unto him, to shew unto his servants things which must shortly come to pass; and he sent and signified it by his angel unto his servant John: [2] Who bare record of the word of God, and of the testimony of Jesus Christ, and of all things that he saw. [3] Blessed is he that readeth, and they that hear the words of this prophecy, and keep those things which are written therein: for the time is at hand.

Revelation 1:1-3

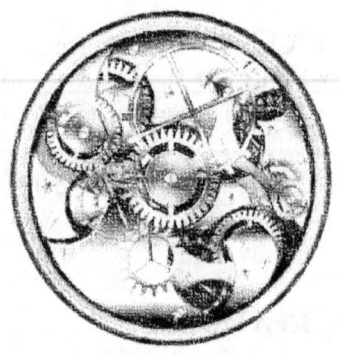

Chapter 15
How Will Time End?

There seems to be collaboration between most books, biblical or mystical, that there is coming some event or dawning, which will take place in the not too distant future. This event is predicted to change the course or evolution of human history. Some believe in the return of extraterrestrials, who they believe, seeded this planet with mankind, thousands of years ago. Others believe in the return of a messiah, unrelated to Jesus Christ, to come at the end of this age and begin a new one. Still others believe in the maturity of the cosmic consciousness of all men (the Force), to sweep this order of things into a new age of conscious oneness, nirvana, or new age. Some believe in a new system (of things) that shall come, facilitating the raising of the soul sleeping dead from the literal grave, to be citizens of a new world government lorded by Jesus Christ.

There are many prophets who have prophesied about the end of the world. Many have been part of religious and Christian groups, but not all. Some predictions have been posted by individuals within a religious group. Some forecast have been endorsed by all a of a groups' adherents, while some predictions emanating from a particular group may not be the belief of the whole. To see, over the centuries, as of yet, none of the end-of-the-world predictions and calculations of any group have been fulfilled. This does not take away from sound biblical interpretation and prognostication of end time events. Many have posted accurate map pins of where the bible says humanity is on God's calendar. The problem lies with pinpointing the exact date of the end itself. Jesus Himself declared in scripture, that in His humanity, not even He knows the date of the end (or understood as the beginning of the end).

The Bible does teach that there will be an ending of this age or *dispensation*. It also teaches there have been many dispensations. We are now in the *Dispensation of Grace* where God's arm is open wide to all who will willfully come to Him and accept His plan of salvation. This is the salvation that has been bought and brought by the crucified and risen Jesus Christ.

Most Christians await the second advent of Christ, but not all agree on how he shall return. *Pretribulationist* interpret that Jesus Christ will return to earth and set up an earthly kingdom in Jerusalem for one thousand years. However, before he does, there will be an event called the *rapture,* in which the dead that died in Christ (who have accepted Him as the way of salvation) will rise again. At the same time all who are alive and have accepted His plan of salvation will be caught up (transformed and transported) in the air to meet the Lord. These believers will go to live with Him in heaven for seven years (the interpretation varies with the timeline). Jesus will return with these followers and reign as King of kings on the earth. After the one thousand years are finished, the final judgment will come. All the dead (these will be the dead who did not accept Christ as Savior) will rise to be judged together with all who have rejected Jesus as being Lord. They will be cast away from God into the *Lake of Fire* along with the Devil, the Anti-Christ, and his *false prophet* who deceived those who are lost. Here is an interesting verse from the Bible concerning this very subject.

Revelations 22:8. But the fearful, and unbelieving, and abominable, and murderers, and whoremongers, and sorcerers, and idolaters, and all liars, shall have their part in the lake which burneth with fire and brim-stone: which is the second death.

Chapter 16
Can the Future Be Changed?

God Almighty knows and holds the future. He knows every event that shall ever happen. He knows the right and wrong decisions you and I make. He knows those who accept and those that reject Him. God has also predestined a place for each group of people. He has made certain promises that are waiting for those who accept Him and He reveals certain promises for those who reject Him

There is an infamous poem called Paradise Lost (1667 by John Milton) that details the events of time from Eden to Judgment. It unfolds the personalities that are involved in the pivots of time. The poem, like the Bible, has a beginning and a definite end. However, what is lost in the poem is the hope for the individual. It is true the borders of the future have been set. God even has angels in places that have been set in place for eons, for one appointed moment to unfold His will. However, in this permanency of time and fate rest a caveat.

There is scripture that says "now faith is" (Hebrews 11:1). Faith, as long as it can be grasped in that scripture, is in the "now" time frame. And accordingly, as to the position of the reader and the hearer it can be grasped. (This is the fact that they are still alive to hear or to read.) The future, whereas it is ultimate, has been set. There is a beginning and an ending. There is a creation and a judgment. However, an individual's place in this future is as changeable as the last word in this sentence. As long as there is breath in a person's body and there is the ability to grasp and receive God's predestined course by faith, the future for that individual can be changed. And, when the future of that individual has been changed, his world and his future have been changed.

He that observeth the wind shall not sow; and he that regardeth the clouds shall not reap. 5 As thou knowest not what is the way of the spirit, nor how the bones do grow in the womb of her that is with child: even so thou knowest not the works of God who maketh all.6 In the morning sow thy seed, and in the evening withhold not thine hand: for thou knowest not whether shall prosper, either this or that, or whether they both shall be alike good.

Chapter 17
Predictions from the Church

As mention in an earlier chapter, there are many belief systems, cultures, groups and individuals that claim the ability to predict the future. These beliefs stretch from the ancient predictions of the *Mayans Indians*, to *Nostradamus's* (1503-1566) predated prophecies, to the tabloid prognostications of American astrologer *Jean Dixon* (mid to late 1900), and to the 21st century Judgment Day predictions of the Oaklyn California based *Family Radio*. Even the Farmer's Almanac has had some amazingly accurate forecasts of changes in global weather. However, most intriguing are the written and current prophecies signed by God Himself through the Holy Spirit.

The Bible is one big prophetic book. It also contains history and messages that are addressed to the people living at a particular time. Still even these messages reach out and seem to manipulate history and time itself. The books in the Bible are good for reaching into the future and bringing the future into the present. It does the same thing with time past. When you read the Bible, in some places, it appears that time itself is just a chessboard for eternity to express itself. The Bible was written by some forty people many of whom had little or no relationship with each other. The time periods of these writers range over four thousand years. However, each book and chapter is somehow woven together as if it were the work of one writer.

Having the ability to predict the future or prophesy also unveils time past. It also is the ability to see what is hidden around the corner of the photograph framed in time. God is omnipotent and He knows all. God does not predict the future. He sees the future as well as the past and present. He is as someone sitting on the hub of giant wheel. The spokes are time—past, present, and future. Eternity is where He sits.

Prophecies that come from the prophets of God are God's revelation of one of the spokes of the wagon wheel. The prophet who is on another spoke receives this revelation, and as directed by God, may speak or write it for someone living on an entirely different spoke. When a prophet speaks a revelation from God, it is God's signature that He—God, is and is in control.

It is also His authorization or warning to believe what He says, so that life adjustments can be made. It is also a revelation of the love of God for His children. A prophecy is also a warning from God to correct behavior or lifestyle. It is also a view into eternity to acknowledge that eternity (ultimate) future will certainly come to pass.

How does this fit in with a person's ability to choose? Simply, the all-knowing God knows the choices made. He is the only being who makes the claim of being all-knowing and therefore is the only one who can prophesy. Again, this is not a prediction, it is a revelation.

God empowers His people through the Holy Spirit. According to scripture, the Holy Spirit is equal with God and shares the same title and authority as God the Father and God the Son–Jesus Christ. Even today, in the New Testament church, empowerment by the Holy Spirit still exist. One way the Holy Spirit empowers is through gifts. These gifts work by His imparting of His knowledge into His chosen vessel (person). This impartation is often called the gifts of the Spirit or Holy Spirit. There are nine gifts.

The Word of Knowledge – revelation of a future event for an individual, family, church, city nation etc.

The Word of Wisdom – revelation of a divine plan or course of action for an individual, family, church, city, nation etc.

The Discerning of Spirits – revelation of the influence or presence of a spirit whether that be God, angel, demon or Satan or an human element in the life of an individual, family, home, church, city, nation, place, worship service or gathering etc.

The Gift of Tongues – Supernatural manifestation of another language, unknown to the believer, imparted by the Holy Sport but exercised by the free will of the individual. This demonstration it is often a prelude of the gift of the *Interpretation of Tongues*. The operation of these two gifts together usually proclaims a prophetic word to the church or an individual. Also, this is not to be confused with another manifestation of speaking tongues by a Christian. This other evidence of tongues is for prayer purposes and though still having its manifestation by the Holy Spirit, is available to all believers. And once received from God, it can also be initiated by the believer's own will.

The Gift of Interpretation of Tongues – used in conjunction with the *Gift of Tongues*. Sometimes the same person will speak the tongue and immediately interpret. Other times, one person will speak the tongue and another will interpret. Still, the Holy Spirit imparts both events.

The Gift of Prophecy – A message of encouragement or correction from God to an individual, family, home, church, city, nation, place, worship service or gathering etc.

The Gift of Healings – A supernatural impartation from the Holy Spirit to heal diseases; It is plural because of the variety in the way this gift manifests itself. The Holy Spirit may have healing of a certain diseases predominate in the ministry of a particular believer. The manifestation of this gift is not necessarily the same as Faith Healing.

The Gift of Faith – This is a supernatural imparting of faith from the Holy Spirit. It is usually beyond the believed realm of faith that a Christian would have by adhering to and trusting God's Word. This gift might be identified with raising the dead or walking on water.

The Gift of the Working of Miracles – This imparting from the Holy Spirit is a supernatural performance of miracles that are beyond the laws of nature. Some association of this gift may be seen in feeding the multitudes with a little food; or in stopping a storm.

This gift is special and has often been the help for multitudes throughout the ages. It is not necessarily God's best way of intervention. This gift does not take the place of the manifestations of God that come from trusting Him and His Word every day.

As listed above, the gifts that are mostly associated with prophecy or future telling are the gift of tongues, the gift of interpretation of tongues, the gift of prophecy, the gift of the word of knowledge, and the gift of the word of wisdom. These gifts have a test for authentication. They can only be given by the Holy Spirit and can only come to a person who has a saving relationship with God through Jesus Christ. These gifts are never to supersede God's written Word. Their purposes are to demonstrate God's love to people, glorify God, and bring people into closer relationship with Him. They are never given to deceive, bewitch or bring attention to the person operating in these gifts. These gifts are to be under the scrutiny of the authority of the church.

Then Paul stood in the midst of Mars' hill, and said, Ye men of Athens, I perceive that in all things ye are too superstitious. [23] For as I passed by, and beheld your devotions, I found an altar with this inscription, TO THE UNKNOWN GOD. Whom therefore ye ignorantly worship, him declare I unto you. [24] God that made the world and all things therein, seeing that he is Lord of heaven and earth, dwelleth not in temples made with hands; [25] Neither is worshipped with men's hands, as though he needed any thing, seeing he giveth to all life, and breath, and all things; [26] And hath made of one blood all nations of men for to dwell on all the face of the earth, and hath determined the times before appointed, and the bounds of
Their habitation;

Acts 17:22-26

Chapter 18
Somebody Messed With The Soup

It has been published in this book that the future is not based on a prediction of the future. It is based on choices that are made and on the belief of presented information. If someone is presented a message of a pending future and believes and embraces it, then that prediction will become true. We have discussed that in some cases insight into one's destiny may be a warning to make different choices to change an outcome.

We have seen that the higher the authority of any message believed will be the one that will win out in a person's life. There is no higher authority than God. There is no higher revelation of God's will than His Word. When a person chooses to believe what God says, embraces it, believes it and begins to speak it, a different journey in life begins.

In a stage play, the author chooses the premise of the script. The characters vary in their personalities and placing in the story. There is usually room for diversity in how the actor portrays a role, but the play must always hold to original intent. How each individual acts out their roles in each scene of life will vary respective to personalities and circumstances. Still, the overall future of every individual has a common and ultimate destination. These *ultimate futures* are predestined and cannot be changed. A person choosing God's plan of life will experience God's plan of life. He will experience all that is included in this package including eternal security. Those who do not choose God's plan will have an ultimate destiny apart from God, which will ultimately end up in Hell.

How then do we answer when we have embraced the roads of our ultimate destiny and futures and other things creep in? What about that promotion or raise that didn't seem to come? What about that money for that bill that didn't seem to come before they took the house? What about the mate you prayed about but who married someone else? What about future choosing then?

It's like the pot of soup simmering that you made from scratch. You followed the recipe to the letter, but when you set down to enjoy a bowl, the taste was not what you expected. You don't throw away the soup. You investigate. Perhaps you missed an item somewhere on the menu. Recheck the spices. Were they correct? Were they fresh? Maybe you left the pot on too long and burned the soup slightly. Maybe you didn't leave the soup on long enough to let the flavor blend. Some soup tastes better the next day when the spices have had time to break down. Or perhaps while you left the room for a moment, someone else added something to the soup.

People are always trying to influence us. People are always trying to enforce their will or words on us. Remember that God has given you a say in your life. You do not have to settle for the soup or scoop someone else wants you to follow. You definitely do not have to take or accept the road of doom or destruction. Remember Adam and Eve in the Garden. Why choose knowledge of good and evil when you can choose to walk in God's life?

You have heard this before, and it's true; never give up. Never play a baseball game of nine innings, just keep playing until you win. There may be disappointment in life but that does not affect your ultimate destiny. When you accept God's plan for your life and trust Him, you have entered into a destiny in which He will never let you fail. With God, even something that may look like a failure from one perspective can be changed into something good from another viewpoint. Also, remember there is war going on between the opposing roads of choice. Stand your ground and follow God's way; don't get swept away by the opposite wind. Jesus said it is the one who endures to the end that shall be saved.

The fact that you are reading this book is proof you are alive. If you are alive you have the right to choose. Even the person who may be incarcerated has a right to choose and change. Even the one who is facing a seemingly hopeless situation has the right to choose and change. Even the one, who for whatever reason may have been told he's facing his last breath today or tomorrow has the right to choose life or death, blessing or curse.

You have to start somewhere. I have started for you. I am predicting your future. If you would choose the life of God, your life will never be the same. This is the guarantee that your ultimate destiny and future will be secure. God will deliver you from any pending forecast of doom in your life. If you are oppressed or depressed I call for your freedom now. I speak to any negative influence in your life to leave you alone. Suicide is never the answer. Remember the only escape from the destiny of the future is choice.

Even when it seems to be no way out and it's the last glance at a twenty-foot tsunami wave on the edge of the shore. The power of choice sets us in a whole other realm of sensibility and responsibility. Ours is not always to figure the way out, but to choose the right to have it. Always choose to believe God to give a way of escape. The power rests in the right to trust God beyond all insurmountable odds and that choice rest in the trust that God is able to resurrect the dead. Jesus on the cross before he hung his head to die chose to believe. He said, "Father into your hands I commend (entrust) my spirit"

Chapter 19
How To Predict Your Future
Step by Step

1. Understand that divine order and destiny has put this book into your hands.
2. Realize you have a future no matter what. There is a good destiny to be had.
3. See the whole picture. Understand that you are part of that picture.
4. Understand you have a major part in the future and that nobody can live your life but you
5. Understand the future is based on choices.
6. Get a Bible. If you don't have one, some of the verses are printed out in the back of this book.
7. Find these verses: St. John 3:16 and Romans 10:9-10 (see: Reference Section)
8. Ask God to open your eyes to the truth of your future.
9. Ask God to reveal Jesus Christ to you now.
10. Accept His future for you. (You have a choice.)
11. Pray the prayer on the next page and believe and receive this free gift.
12. Write to the publisher of this book for more details-free.

For I know the thoughts that I think toward you, saith the LORD, thoughts of peace, and not of evil, to give you an expected end.
Jeremiah 29:11

How to Predict Someone Else's Future

If this book has opened a window to your life for fresh air to come in, please share it with someone else. Let's keep this going. If you will do this then you have become the predictor of someone else's future.

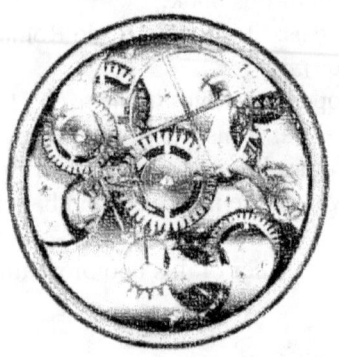

Chapter 20
A Prayer

God in heaven, I believe that You, through Your divine planning, have put this book into my hands. My reading this book is not by chance. God, I found out that there is a future to be had. I found out that you are the only one that truly knows my future because you have given it to me. I have read where you have a wondrous future in store for me, despite any present negative circumstance that may be in my life.

God, I realize that in order to begin the future You have for me, I must first have a relationship with You. I understand that having a relationship with you is my divine purpose.

I have read and now believe Jesus Christ is the only way to come to you and to be in relationship with you. I believe Jesus Christ is the Son of God sent to earth for all mankind. God, I receive what Jesus did on the cross as the ultimate sacrifice for my sins. He took my place and paid the penalty of my disobedience and sin. Now by faith I ask Jesus to come into my heart and be my Savior and Lord. I receive Him now. God your Word declares that if I believe in Jesus I will be saved—*born again* and become an heir to Your kingdom. Thank you Father God for what you have done through Jesus.

Father, I turn my back on sin. I turn my back on the works of darkness. I repent of and turn my back on consultation with any other form of fortune telling. I receive You as the God and Lord of my future.

I thank you right now for the ministry of the Holy Spirit. I thank You that the Holy Spirit has come to (literally) live in me and help me. I receive this wonderful language of prayer that comes from you.

And he said unto them, It is not for you to know the times or the seasons, which the Father hath put in his own power. [8] But ye shall receive power, after that the Holy Ghost is come upon you: and ye shall be witnesses unto me both in Jerusalem, and in all Judaea, and in Samaria, and unto the uttermost part of the earth.

Acts 1:7, 8

Chapter 21
Definitions and Expositions

The following are further definitions of words, phrases and terminology used in this book. Some definitions listed are not discussed, but will be helpful in future predicting.

Angels——spirit beings, messengers of a servant class, originally created to carry out the holy will of God. Some are winged and others are not. Excel in strength over man. Do not have the right to choose. Separate in spiritual class from men; therefore, angels are not the spirits of deceased humans.

Astral projection——the practice or belief that the human spirit can leave the body and travel about at will. Also done with the assistance of a spirit guide.

Born Again——the supernatural act that translates a human being who is a sinner (one who has not embraced Christ as savior and is therefore bound for Hell) into a child of God and a Christian. This transformation comes from a simple yet life-surrendering reception of Jesus Christ's crucifixion and bodily resurrection. The term is also synonymous with

Saved, Child of God, Born from above, Justified, Righteous, Saint.

***The* Bible**——a love story; manual and textbook for Life and eternal life; a contract, testimonial or deed for successful living from God. Written by *Holy* Ghost writers picked and dictated to by God.

Christianity——the doctrine and lifestyle of those Christians who follow Christ

Christians—— followers of Christ; those who have embraced the claims of the Bible concerning Jesus Christ and have the affirmation of His person and spirit living in them through the Holy Spirit. This affirmation comes from the simple yet life-surrendering reception of Jesus Christ's crucifixion and bodily resurrection. Christians usually demonstrate characteristics of Christ such as unconditional love and forgiveness, often unexplainable joy, public acknowledgment of Christ as their personal savior and good public conduct. Christians are also noted for trusting God and prayer. Christians usually attend church services regularly. In agreement with the profession of Christianity, by a new believer, baptism—a type of initiation is administered.

The label of Christianity it often widely placed. It is attributed to everything from those who profess a general agreement with the beliefs of the bible (as in concept) from those who embrace full line-by-line adherences to the teaching of scripture. Some profess Christianity as to distinguish their beliefs system from the religious teachings of other religious persuasion such s Islam or Buddhism

Other names for Christians include—members of the *Church* or *body of Christ*, born-again, believers, the redeemed, saints. The name Christian was first given t o adherents of the teachings of Christ and the Apostles, in the first century church, in the Greek city of Antioch (in modern day Turkey). The name means followers of the Anointed One. Christians were original called follower of *The Way*. The Christian church is generally recognized in two divisions—Catholics and Protestants. Protestants have multiple denominations.

Clairvoyance——a second sight; use of a medium who forecasts distant happenings through visions; ability to instantly know things about people, places or events that were not previously known by the individual through natural means

Demons——evil spirits, subject to Satan to do his bidding in the deception of mankind *from God*.(unclear) Have the ability to possess people, animals and sometimes objects. They hate humans and are opposed to God, the Gospel of Christ and Christians.

Destiny——a predetermined course of events often held to be an irresistible power or agency

Dispensations——definite periods of time, that are identified by specific characteristics of humanity. Also, time periods of specific interactions of God with mankind.

Divining or Divination——The perceived ability of a person through supernatural disclosure to discern an event through the use of intuition, location of an object (like water) or recognize the calling of another person's destiny. This disclosure is not authored by God but by demonic forces sometimes through the use of various natural, psychological, and other techniques.

ESP——(extrasensory perception) perception (as in telepathy, clairvoyance, and precognition) that involves awareness of information about events external to the self not gained through the senses and not deducible from previous experience

Eternity——infinite time, a state where time has no effect, immeasurable

False Prophet——a person who claims to be a mouthpiece or spokesperson of God but is not. One who speaks false or unsanctioned messages as from God and in the name of God. One who speaks a message from Satan or self to purposely deceive.

Familiar Spirit——a demon who comes at the call of a witch or wizard; a demon who also has knowledge of the present or future

Fortune telling or future telling (the term used in this book)—the practice of predicting future events and experiences before they have transpired.
Fortune teller—one who claims the ability to tell the future
Future—time that has not yet transpired, time yet to come
God—the actual name is interpreted Elohim, the creator of all things. Eternal in His being (always was and will be); in love with mankind whom He created in His own image and likeness. Swore Himself to the deliverance of man from the grasp of sin and the lordship of the Satan. Elohim has revealed Himself to mankind as the Almighty God, Yahweh (Jehovah), and Adonai (Lord). He has declared Himself to be the savior of all mankind and settled the fact that there is no other. His salvation is manifested in His son (the manifestation of himself) Jesus Christ, a.k.a., the Word of God. God has also authored a book called the Bible through the use of hand-picked human beings (men of God) and preserved it through history for the purpose of having His story told firsthand.
God the Father—revealed as the head of the three-person existence of God (Father, Son—the Word, and Holy Spirit). God, who is spirit, reveals Himself in the patriarchal sense (opposed to matriarchal sense because it is the male part of mankind that holds the sperm and is the progenitor of the race. A mother carries the seed but is the incubator and the host of the seed.) All creation has come forth from God the Father.

The Father is also viewed as the one who gives loves distinct from a mother's love. A mother's love is set because of the umbilical attachment of a mother to her child. A father must reach out his love to his children and if need be go and get them. This is evident because of sin, which severed man's lifeline to God. It is the Father who is also established as the provider and visionary for the family. John 3:16 may be seen as the act of the Father: "God so loved the world that He gave his only begotten Son..."
God the Son, Jesus Christ—God's manifested Son, the person and manifestation of the Word of God, Pre-human existence as the 2nd person

of the three-part existence of God (Father, Son—the Word, and Holy Spirit). Jesus was born as prophesied by a virgin and grew up to become the ultimate and eternal sacrifice for mankind's rebellion.

Jesus completed this task and rose from the dead also as prophesied. This very act fulfilled God's declaration of being the savior of all. Salvation from hell (and a life of hell) has been made available to all who receive by faith what Jesus did on the cross. All the power of Jesus Christ is still usable on earth today against the forces of evil. It is also available for help with the day-to-day circumstances of life to all who embraced his name and word in spirit and truth.

God The Holy Spirit——the third person of the three-part existence of God (Father, Son—the Word, and Holy Spirit). He is often known as the power provider from God. The Holy Spirit is the one who empowered the Old Testament prophets to do great feats. He is the one who actually lives in every true Christian simultaneously and is the power source for the Church of Jesus Christ, which is the collective fellowship of all true believers. He was also the means Jesus Christ used to fulfill His mission on earth. The Holy Spirit is the one who reveals the thoughts of God to true believers. He is the one who was the agent for giving the Word to the men that God used to write the Bible.

Horoscope——prediction of an individual's future usually by an astrologer based on the configurations of the planets, especially at the time of a person's birth

Hypnosis——access to a person's subconscious mind which bypasses the conscious; in this altered state of mind, the hypnotist can implant suggestions that will be carried out by the subject when he returns to the conscious mind.

Illusionist——a person who uses techniques to alter the perception of reality, such as in art or in magic.

Incorporeal——without a body, pertaining to the spirit world.

Medium——a person who claims to be the channel for communication to the deceased or spirits

Metaphysical——the philosophical studies of the nature of beings

Mind Reading——see telepathy

New Age and New Age Movement——Belief that there is coming a unified and heighten consciousness that will be the culmination of all religious system and ideology. This event will bring about the dawning of new day or age where universal peace and harmony will reign. This also suggests a universal purging of all who are unwilling to make this cosmic leap. New Agers believe that these ideas are mapped out in the heavens as expressed in references to the Age of Aquarius.

Occult——dealing with magic, astrology, the mysterious, the supernatural, esoteric ideas, or secret beyond the normal

Ouija Board——a marked board of words, letter and number that uses planchette (a flat heart-shaped, wooden object), believed to be a medium for predicting the future and answering questions.

Palm Reader——one who claims to predict the future by the interpretation of crease lines and other aspects of a client's hand.

Paranormal——not explained by known scientific knowledge

Prayer——in the simplest form it is communication with God. A spirit being (Human) conversing to the supreme spirit being.(fragment) Usually, speaking words to God in the form of thanksgiving, praise, confession or petition. Also acknowledging and speaking the Divine Will (God's Word) back to God. It is most effective when offered with childlike faith; a submissive attitude of heart in the life of a Christian.

Predestination——the doctrine and belief that God has selected individuals throughout time to be saved, therefore he will guide them to salvation regardless of free will. The opposite is applied to those who are lost. Because they have not been predestinated to be saved. God will not guide them to salvation. Another definition explains that it is not individuals who are predestined, but the outcome of the roads of choice they select. One who chooses the narrow road to God will live and experience the full strength of His goodness. The one who chooses the broad road of human effort and pride away from God will ultimately end up in Hell and destruction.

Pyramids——the belief in the cosmic significance of pyramids connecting as far back as ancient Egypt. Belief that pyramids attract cosmic force. Belief that their usage can heighten spiritual consciousness and ability.

Prophecy——the classification or the disclosure of future events (often national or global). Biblically, this revelation of information from God is usually unknown to the mouthpiece, the prophet. When sometimes known by the prophet, the application of the message or the timing of delivery may be the unknown. This gift is performed by the will of God not by the individual's will. It is also the expression of the desire of God to a person, nation or church.

Prophet——mouthpiece or spokesperson of God who discloses prophecy usually through speaking or writing.

Prophetic Destiny——belief that every human has a specific and divine purpose and that no person will have fulfilled their true course in life without engaging and fulfilling God's call and purpose.

Psychic Phenomenon——an observable fact or event marked by nonphysical or supernatural forces and influences

Psychic——sensitive to nonphysical or supernatural forces and influences: marked by extraordinary or mysterious sensitivity, perception, or understanding.

Satan——Previously Lucifer (the shining one), a.k.a., the Devil (slanderer), fallen archangel; once was the number one angel in heaven before rebelling against God and being expelled, with one third of the angelic kingdom in allegiance. Deceived mankind into rebellion against God thereby releasing sin and damnation into the human race; stripped of unhindered power over man at the cross of Christ; will face final judgment and the Lake of Fire at the end of time; currently leads the army of demons and fallen angels in a vain plot to foil the mission of the church to reach the world with the message of the Gospel of Jesus Christ.

Séance——an event held for the purpose of contacting or communicating with the deceased or spirits. Usually performed through the aid of a medium.

Self-Hypnosis——the practice of self-manipulation of the subconscious through suggestion and meditation

Sin——the ingrained seed of disobedience against God and His way. It was unleashed in the Garden of Eden by Adam's initial treason against God. Sin infected all of Adam-the Man's posterity (mankind) and was disposed through the spiritual, psychological and physical bloodline of all men born. Its unleashing perverted the truth of God's Word to the world and allowed a false reality of life. It also allowed and gave way to death. Death was activated on the three levels of man's existence, his spirit, soul and body. This affected everything related to these realms. Sin is not only inherited disobedience (and its penalty), but the disobedience that every human born will commit.

Sin separated and separates man from the presence of God. (It is only in the presence of God that human fulfillment can be completed and experienced.)

Sin was conquered and defeated only through Jesus Christ's death on the Cross. This act was the eternal payment and restitution for the disobedience of man. An individual receives this deliverance from sin and its penalty only by accepting and embracing through faith what Jesus did through His death, burial, and bodily resurrection. (This defines & characterizes the Christian, and nothing else.)

All other acts of Christianity result from becoming a Christian (or born again, redeemed, saved). The same as the fruit of an apple tree is evidence that it is indeed an apple tree. An apple tree produces fruit because it is an apple tree. Placing an apple on the tree does not give it—its name. Likewise, being moral and a Christian are not the same. A person can be outwardly moral, but yet still innately a sinner. Being moral does not satisfy God's requirement for the restitution of sin. Restitution is only through the blood of Christ.

Sonship——the link to a father, either through the natural bloodline or through subjection and honor. The son holds rights and privileges that are unique and bestowed only with sons. Sons are heirs to the wealth of the father. Sonship is not gender defined; therefore, a son can be male or female. In the Bible, sonship accrues to all who have embraced Jesus Christ as Lord and Savior, those who enjoy the same rights and privileges that Jesus shared in His role as Son of God. The Bible says that the believer is an heir and a joint heir with Jesus Christ. Sonship is the hierarchy of relation with God the Father.

Soothsaying——the act of foretelling events

Soothsayer——a person who predicts the future by magical, intuitive, or more rational means

Supernatural——operating not according to the physical world; not pertaining to the physical world but the forces to outside of it.

Tarot Reading——The interpretation of certain cards (Tarot) used for divination and fortune telling.

Telekinesis——the ability to manipulate matter with the mind.

Telepathy——the ability to read the thoughts of humans and animals without words

Witch——a practitioner of magic (black or white) and conductor of spells; a believer of the affect of nature and supernatural forces on humans; one that is credited usually with malignant supernatural powers. A woman practicing black magic often with the aid of a devil or familiar spirit.

Wizard——a sorcerer, magician; a person who seems to perform magic

Ultimate Future——this is the set outcome of all things. It cannot be altered. It is more the outcome of all things, not the everyday paths. It is the one future that has been predestined. The predestination is not the people on the path, but the path itself.

Zodiac——an imaginary band in the heavens centered on the ecliptic that encompasses the apparent paths of all the planets except Pluto and is divided into twelve constellations, each taken for astrological purposes to extend thirty degrees of longitude. It is also a cyclic course. The twelve constellations or signs used as symbols in the astrology. Astrologers used the zodiac to predict characteristics and traits of human being born under the zodiac sign of the month of their birth. The position of other heavenly bodies in the daily sky in relationship to the prevailing sign is used to predict a daily horoscope.

Dreams

(List you dreams here. A dream is not just something you have when you sleep. A dream is a strong desire and passion to pursue when you are awake. Dreams do not override or surpass someone else's dream. A God given dream will reach out to help others.)

_____
_____
_____
_____
_____
_____
_____
_____
_____
_____
_____
_____
_____
_____
_____
_____
_____
_____
_____
_____
_____
_____

Personal Goals—5 Years

(List your personal goals for five years. Five years is sixty months from today's date. Be sure to list goals that you are really ready to attain in this time period. Remember you have to be willing to believe and not give up.)

_____
_____
_____
_____
_____
_____
_____
_____
_____
_____
_____
_____
_____
_____
_____
_____
_____
_____
_____
_____
_____
_____
_____
_____

Personal Goals—2 years

(List your personal goals for two years. Two years is twenty four months from today's date. Be sure to list goals that you are really ready to attain in this time period. Remember you have to be willing to believe and not give up.)

Personal Goals—1 year

List your personal goals for one year. A year is twelve months from today's date. Be sure to list goals that you are really ready to attain in this time period. Remember you have to be willing to believe and not give up.

_____
_____
_____
_____
_____
_____
_____
_____
_____
_____
_____
_____
_____
_____
_____
_____
_____
_____
_____
_____
_____
_____
_____
_____
_____

Plans

(Write your plans for reaching your goals here.)

Every goal needs a plan. The old adage states "if you fail to plan, you have planned to fail." Your plans may include engaging help and support from family and friends. Be systematic with you plans. Goal planning should include some key principles: *Be specific with your goals and with your prayers of faith.* A lot of goals and prayers are not fully achieved or received because they are not specific. If you desire employment and your goal and prayer is 'to just to be working' you may be disappointed when you get hired into a job that does not fulfill your dreams.

1. *Make you goals attainable.* This doesn't mean your goals have to be miniscule or vague. What it means is that you must realize that there may be some time passage that must occur before fulfillment. You may have to be aware that there may be obstacles or mountains in the journey that will have to be moved through God's power.
2. *Set a timeline for achieving your goals.* This is whether they are one year, two year or five year goals. Again, some goals will be lifetime ambitions, but there still needs to be road markers along the way to assure that you are indeed heading in the direction of completion.
3. *Set real measurements for goal completion.* There needs to be measurement of change or fulfillment. If your goal is to love life fully every day. Then schedule some things that express that goal. An example may be taking a walk every day and thanking God for every good thing you see on along the path. Another example for this goal—is to find someone who needs hope and encourage them daily until they find their way.

If your goal is to become financially wealthy then began to set up saving and investment strategies to get you there. There are always things to do no matter how small.

4. *Always know the finish line or goal line.* A real goal will always have a tangible evidence of completion. If your goal is to be an 'encourager of people' in three months, then within three months you should have a report or testimony from people whose lives you have blessed.

Although the above references are not in order, many Life Coaches as well as other professionals utilize these principles in something called **S.M.A.R.T Goals**. Smart, as a word, definitely defines this goal process, but the acronym itemizes goals that are **S**pecific, **M**easureable, **A**ttainable, **R**ealistic and **T**ime limited. Following this goal fulfilling system will go a long way in helping you to fulfill your life purpose.

Real Life Decisions

On these pages write major decisions and commitments you have made. These are more than just New Year's resolution. These decisions are those that will affect your lifestyle positively. They can be radical and seem almost impossible to keep.

Remember you can't follow this road on your own. Real life decisions may take help from others but they will definitely need help from God.

_____
_____
_____
_____
_____
_____
_____
_____
_____
_____
_____
_____
_____
_____
_____
_____
_____
_____
_____
_____
_____
_____
_____
_____
_____

Decisions for Forgiveness

Although the topic of *forgiveness* is not discussed in this book, it is necessary in predicting the future. Not *forgiving* will hold you in the past despite your highest dreams or aspirations. The power to *forgive* is in *your* mouth and in *your* heart. It doesn't depend on the apologies of the offender. *Forgiveness* is a decision of heart, not based on feelings or emotions, but on the power of choice. Always ask God to help you, hold you, and heal you. Always make a decision to let the offense go and keeping reminding yourself of your decision.

Write on these pages the specific names, including yourself if applicable, of those who have offended you. Write the date that you made the choice to forgive. If you plan to share this book, you may want to write the names in your personal journal.

_____
_____
_____
_____
_____
_____
_____
_____
_____
_____
_____
_____
_____
_____
_____
_____
_____

Affirmations and Confessions

Write on these pages confessions or affirmations that you have learned out of this book. Write positive words or scriptures that you know will lead you and push you into your future. Remember, the powers of words are number one in predicting your future. This is expressed by believing those words, speaking those words, and acting on those words. The greatest words are those that come from the mouth of God Himself found in the Holy Scripture.

Date You Accepted God's Plan For Your Life
(Pray the prayer on page 83)

It is a good thing to remember the date or relative date that you prayed this prayer with total faith in God. When oppression, depression, fear, worry, thoughts of loneliness, or grief try to surround you, go back and find the date that you took this faith step. Remember your good future is sealed in this prayer.

Find a good church in which to fellowship and grow up spiritually. The next step is to get baptized. Simply put, baptism is like an initiation into God's family and He requires it. A *good* church will be able to provide the sacraments for baptism.

_____

Prayer List

List here things in your life that you are praying to God about. Include spiritual growth goals as well as prayer for people, places and things. Please note that prayer is not just asking God for things, but thanking Him for your life and what He is doing in your life. You can always find something good to be thankful for—if you try.

Let your thanksgiving take you to a place where you are worshipping God. When you worship God you are bowing before Him (although it is often good to do this physically, God desires foremost the obeisance of your heart). When you worship, you are identifying that He is greater than all—including yourself and your situations. Worship can be as simple as saying Father God I love you.

It also important to remember that prayer is talking to God. However, the best way to get answers to your prayers is to find the answers first in His Word the Holy Bible.

Biblical Promises

This will require some homework on your part. The Bible list a multitude of precious promises (2 Peter 1:2-4) that God has given to His children. Search the Holy Bible and find scriptures that pertain to your life. When you find them—pray and believe them. Below is only a sample. The verses listed are from the New King James Version.

Life
Psalms 103:1-5

Bless the LORD, O my soul; And all that is within me, *bless* His holy name!
^{2} Bless the LORD, O my soul, And forget not all His benefits:
^{3} Who forgives all your iniquities, Who heals all your diseases,
^{4} Who redeems your life from destruction, Who crowns you with loving kindness and tender mercies,
^{5} Who satisfies your mouth with good *things, So that* your youth is renewed like the eagle's.

Deuteronomy 30:19

I call heaven and earth as witnesses today against you, *that* I have set before you life and death, blessing and cursing; therefore choose life, that both you and your descendants may live;

Psalms 91:14-16

^{14} Because he hath set his love upon me, therefore will I deliver him: I will set him on high, because he hath known my name.
^{15} He shall call upon me, and I will answer him: I will be with him in trouble; I will deliver him, and honour him.
^{16} With long life will I satisfy him, and shew him my salvation.

Proverbs 18:21
Death and life are in the power of the tongue, And those who love it will eat its fruit.

1 John 5:12
He who has the Son has life; he who does not have the Son of God does not have life.

1 John 5:13
These things I have written to you who believe in the name of the Son of God, that you may know that you have eternal life, and that you may continue to believe in the name of the Son of God.

John 3:16
For God so loved the world that He gave His only begotten Son, that whoever believes in Him should not perish but have everlasting life.

Freedom from Fear
2 Timothy 1:7
For God has not given us a spirit of fear, but of power and of love and of a sound mind.

Romans 8:15
For you did not receive the spirit of bondage again to fear, but you received the Spirit of adoption by whom we cry out, "Abba, Father."

1John 4:18
There is no fear in love; but perfect love casts out fear, because fear involves torment. But he who fears has not been made perfect in love.

Freedom from Satan, Demons, Darkness
Luke 10:19

Behold, I give unto you power to tread on serpents and scorpions, and over all the power of the enemy: and nothing shall by any means hurt you.

Isaiah 54:17

No weapon that is formed against thee shall prosper; and every tongue that shall rise against thee in judgment thou shalt condemn. This is the heritage of the servants of the Lord, and their righteousness is of me, saith the Lord

Northing Impossible with God
Mark 11:22-25

For assuredly, I say to you, whoever says to this mountain, 'Be removed and be cast into the sea,' and does not doubt in his heart, but believes that those things he says will be done, he will have whatever he says.
[24] Therefore I say to you, whatever things you ask when you pray, believe that you receive *them,* and you will have *them.*

Hope
Jeremiah 29:11

For I know the thoughts that I think toward you, says the LORD, thoughts of peace and not of evil, to give you a future and a hope.

Protection & Safety
Psalm 91

¹ He who dwells in the secret place of the Most High shall abide under the shadow of the Almighty.

² I will say of the LORD, *"He is* my refuge and my fortress; My God, in Him I will trust."

³ Surely He shall deliver you from the snare of the fowler *and* from the perilous pestilence.

⁴ He shall cover you with His feathers, and under His wings you shall take refuge; His truth *shall be your* shield and buckler.

⁵ You shall not be afraid of the terror by night, nor of the arrow *that* flies by day,

⁶ *Nor* of the pestilence *that* walks in darkness, *Nor* of the destruction *that* lays waste at noonday.

⁷ A thousand may fall at your side, and ten thousand at your right hand; But it shall not come near you.

⁸ Only with your eyes shall you look, and see the reward of the wicked.

⁹ Because you have made the LORD, *who is* my refuge, *even* the Most High, your dwelling place,

¹⁰ No evil shall befall you, nor shall any plague come near your dwelling;

¹¹ For He shall give His angels charge over you, to keep you in all your ways.

¹² In *their* hands they shall bear you up, lest you dash your foot against a stone.

¹³ You shall tread upon the lion and the cobra, the young lion and the serpent you shall trample underfoot.

[14] "Because he has set his love upon Me, therefore I will deliver him; I will set him on high, because he has known My name.
[15] He shall call upon Me, and I will answer him; I *will be* with him in trouble; I will deliver him and honor him.
[16] With long life I will satisfy him, and show him My salvation."

Acts 2:21
And it shall come to pass that whoever calls on the name of the LORD Shall be saved.

Healing
Proverb 7:20-23
My son, give attention to my words; Incline your ear to my sayings.
[21] Do not let them depart from your eyes; Keep them in the midst of your heart;
[22] For they *are* life to those who find them, And health to all their flesh.
[23] Keep your heart with all diligence, For out of it *spring* the issues of life.

Matthew 8:16-17
When evening had come, they brought to Him (Jesus) many who were demon-possessed. And He cast out the spirits with a word, and healed all who were sick, [17] that it might be fulfilled which was spoken by Isaiah the prophet, saying:" *He Himself took our infirmities And bore our sicknesses.* "

Salvation
Romans 10:9-10
That if you confess with your mouth the Lord Jesus and believe in your heart that God has raised Him from the dead, you will be saved. [10] For

with the heart one believes unto righteousness, and with the mouth confession is made unto salvation.

Salvation for Eternity
1 John 5:11-13

And this is the testimony: that God has given us eternal life, and this life is in His Son.

[12] He who has the Son has life; he who does not have the Son of God does not have life.

[13] These things I have written to you who believe in the name of the Son of God, that you may know that you have eternal life, and that you may *continue to* believe in the name of the Son of God.

Family Relationships
Ephesians 6:1-4

Children, obey your parents in the Lord, for this is right. [2] *"Honor your father and mother,"* which is the first commandment with promise: [3] *"that it may be well with you and you may live long on the earth."* [4] And you, fathers, do not provoke your children to wrath, but bring them up in the training and admonition of the Lord.

Psalms 27:10

[10] When my father and my mother forsake me, Then the LORD will take care of me.

Freedom from Suicide & Depression
John 8:32

And you shall know the truth, and the truth shall make you free."

John 8:36

Therefore if the Son makes you free, you shall be free indeed.

Having Relationship with God
Galatians 4:6

And because you are sons, God has sent forth the Spirit of His Son into your hearts, **cry**ing out, "Abba, **Father!**"

1 John 1-4

That which was from the beginning, which we have heard, which we have seen with our eyes, which we have looked upon, and our hands have handled, concerning the Word of life

[2] the life was manifested, and we have seen, and bear witness, and declare to you that eternal life which was with the Father and was manifested to us

[3] that which we have seen and heard we declare to you, that you also may have fellowship with us; and truly our fellowship *is* with the Father and with His Son Jesus Christ.

[4] And these things we write to you that your joy may be full.

1 John 3

Behold what manner of love the Father has bestowed on us, that we should be called children of God! Therefore the world does not know us, because it did not know Him.

Matthew 6:8-14

"Therefore do not be like them. For your Father knows the things you have need of before you ask Him. [9] In this manner, therefore, pray:

Our Father in heaven, Hallowed be Your name.

[10] Your kingdom come. Your will be done on earth as *it is* in heaven.

[11] Give us this day our daily bread.

[12] And forgive us our debts, as we forgive our debtors.

[13] And do not lead us into temptation, but deliver us from the evil one. For Yours is the kingdom and the power and the glory forever. Amen.
[14] "For if you forgive men their trespasses, your heavenly Father will also forgive you. [15] But if you do not forgive men their trespasses, neither will your Father forgive your trespasses.

Matthew 7:11
[11] If you then, being evil, know how to give good gifts to your children, how much more will your Father who is in heaven give good things to those who ask Him!

Having Relationship with People
Matthew 19:19
'Honor your father and your mother,' and, 'You shall love your neighbor as yourself.'

Romans 13:8
Owe no one anything except to love one another, for he who loves another has fulfilled the law.

Romans 13:9
For the commandments, "You shall not commit adultery," "You shall not murder," "You shall not steal," "You shall not bear false witness," "You shall not covet," and if there is any other commandment, are all summed up in this saying, namely, "You shall love your neighbor as yourself."

Luke 10:25-37

[25] And behold, a certain lawyer stood up and tested Him, saying, "Teacher, what shall I do to inherit eternal life?"

[26] He said to him, "What is written in the law? What is your reading of it?" [27] So he answered and said, "'You shall love the LORD your God with all your heart, with all your soul, with all your strength, and with all your mind,' and 'your neighbor as yourself.'"

[28] And He said to him, "You have answered rightly; do this and you will live."

[29] But he, wanting to justify himself, said to Jesus, "And who is my neighbor?"

[30] Then Jesus answered and said: "A certain man went down from Jerusalem to Jericho, and fell among thieves, who stripped him of his clothing, wounded him, and departed, leaving him half dead.

[31] Now by chance a certain priest came down that road. And when he saw him, he passed by on the other side.

[32] Likewise a Levite, when he arrived at the place, came and looked, and passed by on the other side.

[33] But a certain Samaritan, as he journeyed, came where he was. And when he saw him, he had compassion.

[34] So he went to him and bandaged his wounds, pouring on oil and wine; and he set him on his own animal, brought him to an inn, and took care of him.

Romans 13:9

For the commandments, "You shall not commit adultery," "You shall not murder," "You shall not steal," "You shall not bear false witness," "You shall not covet," and if there is any other commandment, are all summed up in this saying, namely, "You shall love your neighbor as yourself."

[35] On the next day, when he departed, he took out two denarii, gave them to the innkeeper, and said to him, 'Take care of him; and whatever more you spend, when I come again, I will repay you.'

[36] So which of these three do you think was neighbor to him who fell among the thieves?" [37] And he said, "He who showed mercy on him." Then Jesus said to him, "Go and do likewise."

1 Peter 3:8-12

[8] Finally, all of you be of one mind, having compassion for one another; love as brothers, be tenderhearted, be courteous; [9] not returning evil for evil or reviling for reviling, but on the contrary blessing, knowing that you were called to this, that you may inherit a blessing. [10] For "He who would love life and see good days, Let him refrain his tongue from evil, And his lips from speaking deceit. [11] Let him turn away from evil and do good; Let him seek peace and pursue it. [12] For the eyes of the LORD are on the righteous, And His ears are open to their prayers; but the face of the LORD is against those who do evil."

Birthdays, Anniversaries, Special Events

One of the elements in predicting our future is celebrating events, special occasions, seasons and timelines. This is different from worshipping these times or idolatrizing them. Giving thanks for people's lives, as well as our own, not only shows appreciation, but connects us to the whole of life.

If we are going to predict a good day, then why not celebrate in it when it manifest. Congruently, if we are predicting long life, then why not celebrate and be gracious in each day for its place in the journey.

On these pages write special events such as birthdays and anniversaries. Anticipate them not as the fulfillment of hope, but as markers along the way in your celebration of every day that God gives.

Notes

Scripture References

John 3

There was a man of the Pharisees, named Nicodemus, a ruler of the Jews:[2] The same came to Jesus by night, and said unto him, Rabbi, we know that thou art a teacher come from God: for no man can do these miracles that thou doest, except God be with him.

[3] Jesus answered and said unto him, Verily, verily, I say unto thee, Except a man be born again, he cannot see the kingdom of God.[4] Nicodemus saith unto him, How can a man be born when he is old? can he enter the second time into his mother's womb, and be born?

[5] Jesus answered, Verily, verily, I say unto thee, Except a man be born of water and of the Spirit, he cannot enter into the kingdom of God.[6] That which is born of the flesh is flesh; and that which is born of the Spirit is spirit.[7] Marvel not that I said unto thee, Ye must be born again.[8] The wind bloweth where it listeth, and thou hearest the sound thereof, but canst not tell whence it cometh, and whither it goeth: so is every one that is born of the Spirit.[9] Nicodemus answered and said unto him, How can these things be? [10] Jesus answered and said unto him, Art thou a master of Israel, and knowest not these things?[11] Verily, verily, I say unto thee, We speak that we do know, and testify that we have seen; and ye receive

not our witness.[12] If I have told you earthly things, and ye believe not, how shall ye believe, if I tell you of heavenly things?[13] And no man hath ascended up to heaven, but he that came down from heaven, even the Son of man which is in heaven.[14] And as Moses lifted up the serpent in the wilderness, even so must the Son of man be lifted up:[15] That whosoever believeth in him should not perish, but have eternal life.[16] **For God so loved the world, that he gave his only begotten Son, that whosoever believeth in him should not perish, but have everlasting life.**[17] **For God sent not his Son into the world to condemn the world; but that the world through him might be saved.**[18] **He that believeth on him is not condemned: but he that believeth not is condemned already, because he hath not believed in the name of the only begotten Son of God.**

[19] And this is the condemnation, that light is come into the world, and men loved darkness rather than light, because their deeds were evil.[20] For every one that doeth evil hateth the light, neither cometh to the light, lest his deeds should be reproved. [21] But he that doeth truth cometh to the light, that his deeds may be made manifest, that they are wrought in God

Romans 10

[8] But what saith it? The word is nigh thee, even in thy mouth, and in thy heart: that is, the word of faith, which we preach; [9] That if thou shalt confess with thy mouth the Lord Jesus, and shalt believe in thine heart that God hath raised him from the dead, thou shalt be saved. [10] For with the heart man believeth unto righteousness; and with the mouth confession is made unto salvation. [11] For the scripture saith, Whosoever believeth on him shall not be ashamed. [12] For there is no difference between the Jew and the Greek: for the same Lord over all is rich unto all that call upon him. [13] For whosoever shall call upon the name of the Lord shall be saved. [14] How then shall they call on him in whom they have not believed

Acts 4

[10] Be it known unto you all, and to all the people of Israel, that by the name of Jesus Christ of Nazareth, whom ye crucified, whom God raised from the dead, even by him doth this man stand here before you whole. [11] This is the stone which was set at nought of you builders, which is become the head of the corner. [12] Neither is there salvation in any other: for there is none other name under heaven given among men, whereby we must be saved

Mark 16

[15] And he (Jesus) said unto them, Go ye into all the world, and preach the gospel to every creature. [16] He that believeth and is baptized shall be saved; but he that believeth not shall be damned.

This book was published by:

The Glory Cloud publications LLC
P.O. Box 193
Sicklerville, NJ 08081
www.theglorycloudpublications.com

For additional information about us and how to obtain other literature
please write to the above address.

*Psalms 68:11
*Habakkuk 2:3,4 *2 Corinthians 1-7
*Jude 22

With our Voice and His Glory, by Faith making a Difference in the World

All biblical scriptures are from the King James Version of the bible unless otherwise noted

www.ingramcontent.com/pod-product-compliance
Lightning Source LLC
Chambersburg PA
CBHW072338300426
44109CB00042B/1667